HERE LYES Y BODY
OF M BELOVED
Y 31st OCTOBER
1690
REST Y IN
CE FOR ALL
ERNITY

Enter If You Dare...

BOOK REVIEWS

Review:

In 1999 a small group of home haunters joined together and sent pictures or video of their home haunts to be compiled into a single VHS tape which was then copied and distributed to the group. This was the start of a tradition that continues today with a set of Haunt DVD's.

I became involved with this project in 2001 when I volunteered to help duplicate the VHS tapes. In 2002 I helped move the set set from VHS to CD's and in 2003 I took over this project and distributed the haunt videos on DVD for the first time. Since then, I have had the honor of compiling the Haunt DVD set each year.

The Haunt DVD's typically have over 100 of the finest home haunts including haunts from every part of the US, Canada and even a few haunts from Germany and England (where Halloween is just starting to become popular).

> **How To Haunt Your House is a masterpiece.**
>
> Halloween Propmaster
> (Paul Venturella)

In addition to compiling the annual Haunt DVD set, I am a serious home haunter myself. I am a founding member of The Rocky Mountain Haunters group and spend all year building props and getting ready for Halloween.

I tell you this so you know that when I tell you how comprehensive, detailed and just flat out helpful, "How To Haunt Your House" is, you will know that I have considerable experience in how I and many, many others haunt their houses.

This book covers a broad range of great props for making your home that one house all the kids talk about, not just at Halloween, but all your long whenever Halloween come up. The house they will tell their children about, "When I was a kid there was this one house that really scared us...."

"How To Haunt Your House" is a masterpiece. The information on exactly what to use and how to use it, explained in a way you will understand and be able to create these props, with detailed pictures, is the best book on the subject I have ever seen.

The Mitchell's (Shawn & Lynne) are award winning home haunters themselves and their efforts to create a book to help others haunt their house have paid off by creating a book no one interested in creating a great Halloween display will want to be without. This book would be valuable to both those like myself with decades of home haunting under their belt as well as those just starting out in Halloween decorating.

Add this book to your library, you will not be sorry!"

**Halloween PropMaster
(Paul Venturella)
www.halloweenpropmaster.com**

Review:

The book looks great! Super visuals, clear-cut instructions... and very well put-together. You do amazing work with the haunt, and the book shows that clearly. I can't wait to see the final print version. (I am SO buying a copy for my collection!!!) Thanks for sharing!!

**Deanna Griffith
Ghostess Deanna
The Dead End
www.howloweenqueen.com
www.floridahaunters.com
www.ghostessdeanna.blogspot.com**

> **Super visuals, clear-cut instructions... and very well put-together.**
>
> Ghostess Deanna
> (Deanna Griffith)

Review:

Brief Overview: A book designed to provide Haunters and Halloween enthusiasts with quality step by step information to enhance their Haunts or Halloween endeavors.

Upon receiving the book in it's entirety, I knew that this was a piece that took much time, insight and planning. It was clear to me that the review of this book would take some time. It's not a book that you throw together and market. It's general flavor was above and beyond. The book is colorful, campy and the entire presentation was user friendly. The text is easy to read. The books images and pics entice me as a Haunter and add a certain feel to the book that Halloween Haunted House addicts so desire.

The content is amazing. Not only does the book offer a thorough

index but the topics included in the first book start out on the ground floor in an easy to understand fashion. All of the content is illustrated with step by step instructions on how to achieve your goal. The book has pointers that outline all of the components of a prop and explains it's features. The language is simple. I find this to be very important. Haunter talk can be understood by a person who has dabbled in this industry for a long time. A beginner should have the ability to navigate through the book and easily understand the lingo. This is the case here.

Speaking of books and magazines, I would most likely be excited to see what's to come. I feel that all of the Halloween Haunted House books and magazines are insightful but I'm partial to this one because it's not a sales pitch. It doesn't give you bits and pieces of information that are stretched out and have sole intention on advertising. The information you seek is the

> **Without hesitation, I give this book a 5/5 star rating.**
>
> Pete Henderson
> hauntspace.com founder

information you will find. From speaking to the author(s) I feel that this is one of those books that will be talked about for years to come. I feel that people will want a copy even if it's for pride of ownership. One of the authors Shawn Mitchell (SherlockSam) has been a member of HauntSpace for quite some time and has contributed wonderful knowledge to the community.

All in all, I've had the occasion to read some Haunt books. All of them were interesting. I would prefer not to name the books because I'm speaking of "this" book. I will tell you that some of the books lacked an exciting look and feel. Instead of reading a book that put me in the mood, I found myself feeling like I was back in high school, listening to the typical mono tone voice that went on and on, placing me into a daydream about something else. Teachers of today found that the number one attribute of good teaching is to make the lesson fun, easy to learn and keep the student interested. In my opinion, this has been accomplished with this book. I would probably leaf through the book just to look at the pictures inside because I find it motivational. It's easy to tell that the authors of this book put the project into motion because of their love of Halloween and the Haunted House Industry. Without hesitation, I give this book a 5/5 star rating.

**Pete Henderson
www.hauntspace.com (founder)**

Review:

The Home Haunters Association Team just finished reviewing the soon to be published /How to Haunt Your House/ by Shawn and Lynne Mitchell. The book is a visual feast and a goldmine of information on haunting technique. The book covers a range of topics from basic craft technique through construction of complete props.

The book combines clear writing style with incredibly beautiful photographs depicting prop construction from start to finish. One example is a Celtic tombstone which is so realistic that it includes moss! Another example of well-explained technique is the section on sand casting. The photos and description are so clear that a novice haunter can quickly duplicate complex objects for the haunt. At the book progresses, so does the sophistication of the technique. The section on Pepper's Ghost (the technique used in

> **I would give it five skulls! I'd give it six if that were possible.**
>
> The Home Haunters Association Team

the Ballroom of Disney's Haunted Mansion) make a technique mainly found in commercial haunts accessible to the home haunter. If the book has any shortcoming it is in the discussion of animated props. There's very little on that topic in this volume. However, I understand that there is a second volume in the works and I'll keep my fingers crossed.

All things considered, this book is a masterpiece. I would give it five skulls! I'd give it six if that were possible. I want a hard copy and I'm sure that anyone who considers a home haunt to be more than a pumpkin with a candle in it will want one too!!

The Home Haunters Association Team
http://www.homehauntersassociation.com

How To Haunt Your House

COPYRIGHT

DEADICATION

We were home from Trick-or-Treating by ten, but it felt like two in the morning. Four or five blocks, seemed to be the entire town. Even if there was snow on the ground, it felt like it was 90 degrees. We were never chased down the street by ghosts, werewolves or zombies, but we told everyone we were. One bag of candy was equal to ten, and weighed at least a ton-- or two. Our costumes made us invincible, invisible, or super-scary. There was nothing we couldn't do this one night of the year.

There was one dare, that would give us pause. And one, we each had to take. Palms sweaty, heart racing, we all, in turn, would have to visit the one house, most famous of all... *the* house. The one with the creaky, wood porch, the dimly lit windows, the huge, ominous door which held back unspeakable, untold horrors. Every neighborhood had at least one. The house, where the decorations went beyond the cardboard cutouts and plastic, jack-a-lantern grins. It was *the haunted house*, a carefully, crafted masterpiece of everything that made us want to turn and run. I still remember the cobwebs, the flashing lights, and the fear that someone, or something, was lurking in the shadows behind the hedges. Waiting for us to get close before jumping out! We would scream, then laugh, then argue about who was more scared, my friend, or me.

This book is dedicated to all of us who remember what Halloween was-- and what it *can* be. To all the closet haunters, who dwell in garages, basements, and home-haunt forums, or even in the family dining room, making props all year long, for one single night of the year-- you are the true spirit of Halloween. *Long, may you haunt.* BOO!

How To Haunt Your House
CONTENTS

Basic Tools & Materials
You Can Use For Most Projects

W hether you're a hard core home haunter, a re-crafter of store bought items or looking to create the most spook-tacular party there ever was, there are a few handy tools to have on hand before you start.

1 Craft Paints

Black and white craft paints are essential. Other colors, such as red, brown, green and yellow could also be used.

2 Gauze or Cheesecloth

You'll find many uses for this versatile, light-weight material. It can be dyed, torn, painted and wrapped.

3 Drywall Compound

This is excellent for creating textures on all kinds of props and can be mixed with latex paint for a starting base color. Once dry, it can be painted further and made to resemble everything from marble to wood.

4 Wood Burning Tool

This tool is perfect for sculpting detail into Styrofoam. Different tips can achieve a variety of effects. The heated tool melts Styrofoam quickly, but the results can be everything from chiseled stone to lettering.

5 Craft Brushes

A variety of craft brush sizes are always handy for applying final details to props.

6 Serrated Knife

A serrated knife if useful for cutting Styrofoam. It creates a rough, uneven edge.

7 Craft Glue

Water-soluble craft glue will work for most projects and can be used on Styrofoam.

8 Soldering Tool

An alternative to using a wood burning tool to sculpt Styrofoam is a soldering tool. Use the fine tip for lettering or lay tip on its side for sculpting.

9 Toothpicks

Toothpicks are like straight pins for the home haunter. They are perfect for holding parts in place for a variety of projects in this book. Use the type that is pointed on both ends.

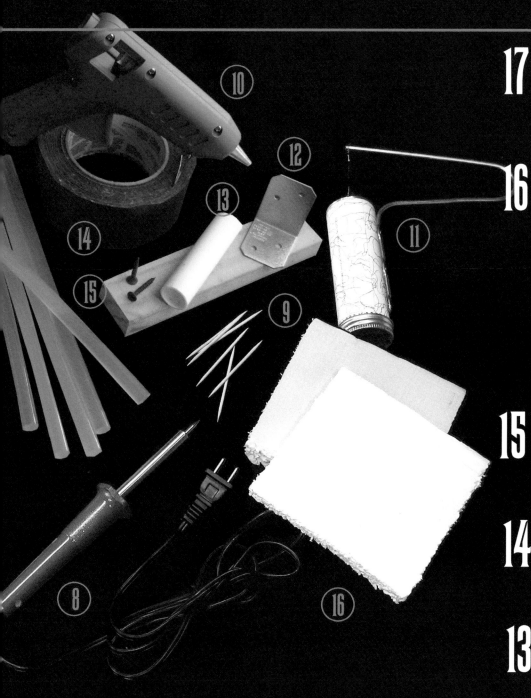

17 Other Useful Items

Carbon paper, black and white spray paint, latex gloves, paver sand, zip ties, fabric dye, wire, wire cutters, PVC cutter, drill & drill bits, wax paper, Plexiglass, carpet glue, rope, pipe installation, spray bottle.

16 Styrofoam

Styrofoam is found in hardware stores and is used as installation in houses. It comes in a variety of thicknesses, from half inch to 2 inches thick. There are two types of Styrofoam. White foam has a larger cell structure and comes in sheets of the largest thickness. Blue (or pink) foam has a tighter composition and is less messy than white foam when cut, but is available only in thinner sizes. Full sheet size is 4 feet by 8 feet. Styrofoam is great for creating large light-weight walls or several tombstones per sheet.

15 Wood & Wood Screws

Excellent for building large prop structures or as interior skeletons of prop characters. Generally 1x2 wood is used. Heavier wood can also be used for extra stability.

14 Duct Tape

An all around useful material in a variety of projects is duct tape. Use to shape a character's body or hold project pieces in place while you work.

13 PVC Pipe

Strong, yet light-weight, PVC is used in making interior, bone structures, fence poles and candle forms. Many sizes and thicknesses are available.

10 Hot Glue Gun & Glue Sticks

The hot glue gun is best tool in the home haunter's arsenal. Have several bags of glue sticks on hand to start with.

11 Heated Wire Cutter

Another tool for cutting and carving Styrofoam is the Wire Styrofoam Cutter. It creates smooth edges.

12 L Brackets

Any wood building projects that use the 1x2 wood will also use lots of L Brackets to join the two pieces of wood together at the corners.

Making Your Own Faux Moss

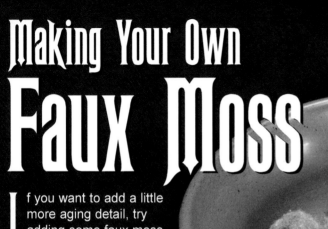

I f you want to add a little more aging detail, try adding some faux moss to your props. It can transform a tombstone so it will seem to have been around for years and years in some dark and spooky graveyard. This recipe is quick and simple and made from materials easily obtained—recycled dryer lint!

1 In a bowl mix a batch of dryer lint with some craft glue and two or more shades of green paint.

2 With a gloved hand, gently mix the lint and liquids until all are moss colored. The paint colors should not mix completely.

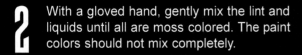

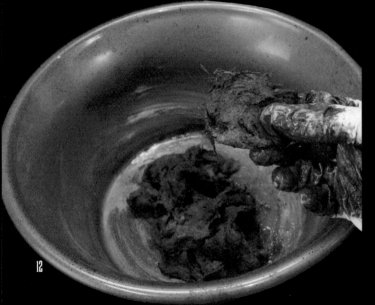

3 Apply pieces of the mixture with your fingers, while it is still wet, by pressing faux moss into the tombstone surface. Let dry. If needed, drybrush some lighter green back on the moss for highlights.

Monster Stamp of Approval

How To Make
Monster Mud

Monster-mud is a term first coined by Steve Hickman of *Terror Syndicate Productions*. However, the recipe and application have been used in the effects industry for some time. It is simple to make and can be applied to an unlimited list of craft projects that require some texture. It also works very well with Styrofoam. The *Monster Mud* creates a textured shell over the light-weight Styrofoam that can then be made to look like a variety of materials. Recycle some of that old paint sitting in the

garage. It doesn't matter what colors you use or mix together. It will be used as a base for other colors on the Styrofoam "stone". How much compound needed depends on the project. Make a large batch in a separate bucket with a lid and you can store it for months. Mix roughly 5 parts drywall compound to 1 part paint and mix. A drywall mixer attached to a drill works best to mix with, but is not necessary. Use latex gloves and protect clothing and surfaces. *Monster Mud* will stain.

Styrofoam buildings and props are meant as decoration only and should not be used in places where the public would come in contact with the structures.

Two sheets of 2 inch thick 4 x 8 Styrofoam form this Abbey entryway. Rough-cut Styrofoam bricks are placed around the opening and in random places on the wall.

Styrofoam Techniques

Styrofoam is light-weight, inexpensive and can be made into all kinds of props or structures. It can be made to resemble crumbling stone, old marble, wood planks, cobble stone, or whatever surface textures are needed.

Cutting a straight edge in Styrofoam requires a ruler and a serrated knife to score the Styrofoam. **1.** First, peel off the any plastic covering from both sides of the Styrofoam. Use the cutting tool to score along the ruler without going all the way through the Styrofoam.

2. Once scored, gently bend away from the score line until the Styrofoam snaps into two clean-edge pieces.

Once the basic shape is cut and a design applied, use any of the heated tools to further shape the Styrofoam. Do this in a well ventilated area and take precautions against fumes. Cracks, holes, lines and text can all be carved into the surface by melting. As the heated tool is pressed into the Styrofoam, the Styrofoam quickly melts away from the hot edges of the tool. Several pieces of Styrofoam can also be layered and glued into place for added depth.

1 Peel plastic from each side of Styrofoam first.

2

Shown here: rounded edge, carved, and cracked stone look

Skull and crossbones sculpted and attached separately

Rough-cut rectangles glued to a larger Styrofoam sheet

Styrofoam "boards" with wood grain drawn in with a hot tool

*Shown here: Cut window-shape glued to larger wall opening.
Separate Styrofoam "bricks" glued around window frame.*

*Shown here:
Rough-cut "bricks"
glued along wall
edge. Styrofoam
"wall" has been
cut in low relief
with a hot tool to
form rounded
"stones".*

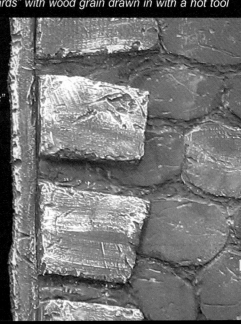

Tombstones look great outside or indoors this time of year. Create a variety of sizes and shapes for best effect. With one large sheet of Styrofoam you could get 4 nice size tombstones made at a fraction of the cost of buying equal sized props that are commercially made.

1 Transfer your pattern to the cut out Styrofoam tomb shape using carbon paper. If the transfer marks are not dark enough, go back over them with a marker.

Making Your Own
Tombstone
Low Relief Style

Make rough, low relief parts, by quickly pressing a heating tool tip straight down into the Styrofoam repeatedly until the surface is lowered.

You will need: 1 cutout Styrofoam tombstone, carbon paper, enlarged template design (*your own, or one found online*), ball point pen, black permanent marker, hot cutting tools of choice, serrated knife, *Monster Mud* (*see page 13*), black and white craft paints (or colors of choice), paint brushes, latex gloves

2 Using a hot tool point, in this case, a soldering tool, go over the pattern lines. Heat melts the Styrofoam instantly, so you will need to keep the tool moving at a quick pace. For more accurate design work, you will need to cut the lines with an X-acto blade.

3 Using a mixture of drywall compound and any color paint, called *Monster Mud* (*see page 13*), apply the mud with a brush to the entire surface of the tombstone. Be sure to cover all sides, letting each side dry completely, before moving on. No Styrofoam should be showing when you are done.

4 When the mud coat is completely dry, paint the raised surfaces with a darker, gray, craft paint and a wet brush. Some of the mud color can be left as is. This will help to achieve a more realistic "stone" color.

5 Once step 4 is dry, paint any carved or low surface areas with black, craft paint and a small brush. This will help the details to stand out.

Note: Mix black and white craft paint to get gray color.

6 Using a dry, wide brush and a small amount of white, craft paint, gently drag the brush over the tombstone surface. High surface details will catch the white paint and finish the "stone" look.

The "stone" look of our completed tombstone is perfect for any graveyard or Halloween setting. To give it an extra, spooky glow... spray it with glow-in-the-dark or blacklight hairspray (see page 24). Shine a blacklight in its direction and your ghostly tombstone really comes alive.

Making Your Own Tombstone
Stone Cross Style

You will need: 1 cutout Styrofoam tombstone, 2 pieces of Styrofoam sized to create base, carbon paper, enlarged template design (*your own, or one found online*), ball point pen, black permanent marker, hot cutting tools of choice, serrated knife, *Monster Mud (see page 13)*, black and white craft paints (or colors of choice), paint brushes, craft glue, toothpicks, latex gloves, faux moss (*see page 12*) (optional)

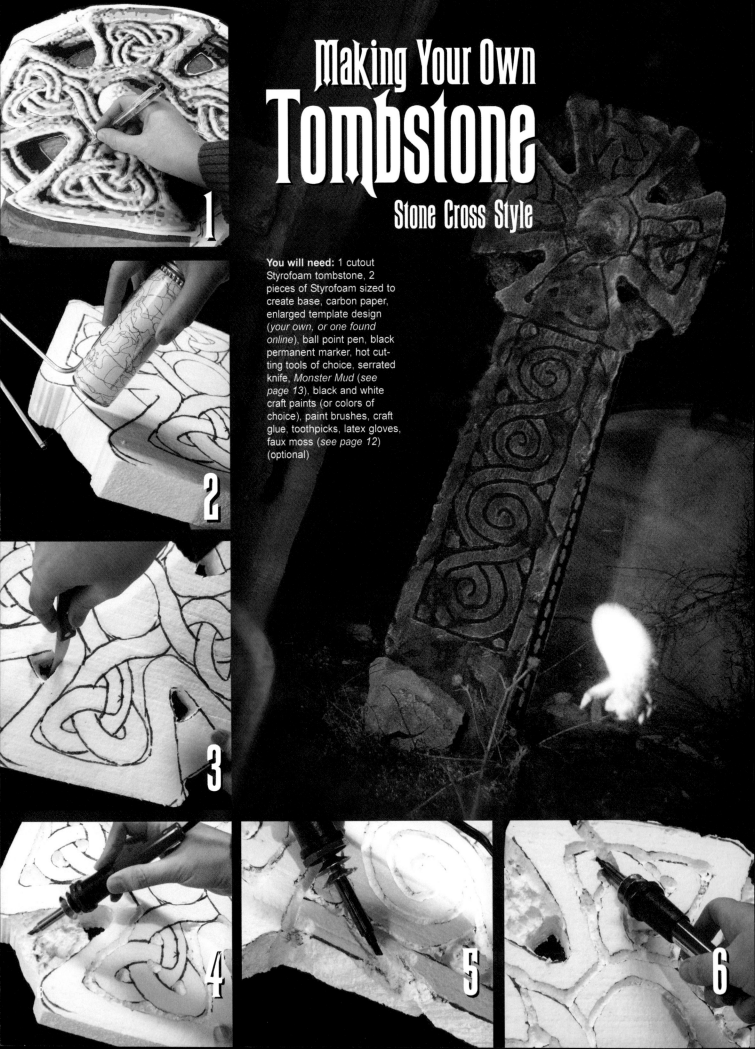

1 Once you have a cross design, cut the cross shape to size out of Styrofoam using a serrated knife. Use carbon paper and ball point pen to transfer the design to the Styrofoam. Retrace the lines with a marker if needed.

2 A heated wire tool can be used to further define the cross edges and smooth out the surface texture.

3 Cut out any openings needed in the design.

4 Using a heated tool with a point, press the side of the tip down to lower parts of the design and to create added interest.

5 Using the side of the heated tool, drag tool to create worn cracks in the cross. Think about how time would wear and tear a real tombstone. Perfect, sharp edges would get chipped or cracked. Make some deeper than others and use a variety of angles.

6 Trace as much as the pattern lines for level of detail, as desired.

7 For the center circle, roughen a Styrofoam circle by melting it into shape. Leave the bottom side flat.

8 Use craft glue and a toothpick to attach the flat side of the circle to the cross.

9 Once all the detail has been created, coat the entire surface with *Monster Mud* (*see page 13*). Use a small brush to get the Mud into all the crevices.

10 For the cross base, glue two sheets of Styrofoam together, using toothpicks to hold in place. To make the cross removable from the base for easier storage, mud and paint separately. Assemble once dry.

11 Trace out the cross bottom edge for cut position.

12 Cut all the way through both layers with a serrated knife. Remove cut center pieces. Add worn details and coat with *Monster Mud*.

Stone Cross Style

Paint darker gray over Monster Mud

Paint in black details

13 With a darker gray than the base coat, add some random brush marks over the top surface of the whole piece.

14 Use a finer brush to add black craft paint into all the lower surface details. This should give the effect of years of dirt having filled in all the cracks and help the design to stand out.

15 With a dry, wider brush use a small amount of white craft paint and lightly drag the brush over the highest surface details.

Drybrush lightly with white, then use a brown wash for grunge

Add faux moss for age

16 Also, drybrush the edges of the tombstone with white.

17 Add some more grunge details with brown, craft paint and a wet brush. Imitate how rain would run the dirt downward and stain.

18 Finally, add faux moss (*see page 12*) to random parts of the stone for more age.

Making Your Own
Tombstone
High Relief Style

You will need: 1 cutout Styrofoam tombstone, 1 piece faux ivy, 2 faux roses with stems (or items of your choice), carbon paper, enlarged template design (*your own, or one found online*), ball point pen, black permanent marker, hot cutting tools of choice, serrated knife, *Monster Mud* (page 13), black, brown and white craft paints (or colors of choice), paint brushes, toothpicks, latex gloves

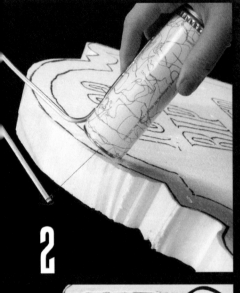

1. Trace your pattern onto the Styrofoam cutout tombstone using carbon paper and ball point pen. Retrace lines with a marker to make them easier to see.

2. Use a hot wire tool to refine and smooth the stone edge.

3. Use a hot tool tip to cut in any letters and details needed.

4. *Monster Mud* (*see page 13*) all sides of the tombstone.

5. Attach faux ivy or roses with stems using a thick coating of *Monster Mud*. Toothpicks can also be used to hold items in place. Let dry.

6. Some parts of the faux ivy and roses can remain above the surface.

7. Go over the over the entire tombstone with a darker shade of craft paint leaving some of the base color showing.

8. Paint black any cut in areas and low level details.

9. Dry brush all the high level surface details. Don't forget to highlight the details such as leaf veins and flower petal edges.

10. Last, add some brown, craft paint washes in a downward motion to simulate years of rain runoff in some areas of the design.

Haunt Tips

Place various size tombstones in a group for more drama.

Add lighting on the tombstone group so the tombstones cast shadows on the ground and other tombstones for a creepier look.

Vary the angles of the tombstones for a decrepit, run down cemetery apperance. Tilt some forward, side-ways or back.

Use tombstones indoors in unexpected places such as a table setting, attached to the backs of chairs, on the buffet, or lined up behind a couch.

10

7

8

9

How To
Make It Glow

Glow-in-The-dark Paint
Glow-in-the-dark paint mixed with water is opaque. White light will "charge" the liquid and cause it to glow for a time or will glow continuously under blacklight.

Highlighter Pens
Remove the inner cartridge of a highlighter pen and soak in water over night. Highlighter Liquid is translucent and seems to glow under normal lighting. It will also glow brightly under blacklight.

Glow Sticks
Once activated, glow sticks will glow for a limited time. Place entire tube inside objects or submersed in other liquids for glow effect.

W hether you are creating a mad scientist lab filled with all sorts of glowing viles and bottles or a cemetery that glows with it's own ethereal light, glow-in-the-dark paints and sprays can give your props that extra special look.

Mixing props using both blacklight and glow-in-the-dark glow colors is also effective.

24

Here lies Billy West
shanty songs

Anything white will glow under blacklight. Glow-in-the-dark paints and sprays will also work with blacklight.

Tennis Ball Fuzz
The yellow fuzz of tennis balls glows brightly under blacklight.

Liquid Starch
Liquid Starch will glow under blacklight. It has a milky appearance. Use to fill laboratory jars or test tubes.

Blacklight Hairspray
Blacklight hairspray is invisible on props except when exposed to a blacklight. It will cast a blue glow. As a spray, it captures surface details easily.

RIT® Fabric Whitener
This product has a translucent glow when exposed to black-light. Great for applying to white fabrics, such as cheesecloth, to make them glow under black-light even more.

Fluorescent Paints
Fluorescent paint comes in a variety of colors. Use to paint in details like eyes, or lettering, or mix with water and use to fill laboratory jars or test tubes.

See page 74 for additional FX lighting information.

25

Marbleizing Props

Turning everyday objects into stone or marble is an easy process. At least two colors are needed to create a marble look. Here, black and white spray paint is used.

1 Paint or spray a base color onto your prop. This base color is black spray paint.

2 Remove nozzle from can. Carefully, widen the nozzle opening with an X-acto knife. Do this for the white and black spray paint nozzles. This will cause the spray to splatter when sprayed.

3 Lightly spray both the white and black at the same time. This gives a nice mixture effect of the two colors.

4 If you want a streaky paint effect, spray in one spot over the still wet paint with a clear varnish until the paint runs. Or, you can hand-paint in streaks afterwards.

Prepare Can Nozzle

2

After removing nozzle, carefully, widen the nozzle opening with an X-acto knife.

3

4

Marbleizing Props

1 Original painted, plaster garden statue.

2 Spray paint entire statue in black.

3 With widened nozzles (*see page 27*), spray on white and black spray paints.

4 Finally, using a dry brush and some black, craft paint, paint only the edges to bring back some of the details.

Add some hot glue spider webs (page 30) or Blacklight hairspray and a Blacklight (page 24) and this prop is ready to go haunting!

You will need: 10 yards or more of cheesecloth or gauze, black, fabric dye, large pot to dye cloth, 2 small nails (*optional*), hammer (*optional*), scissors

Pulling Spider's Web

Cobwebs are the number one requirement for every haunted house decor. The more cobwebs, the more haunted your house will seem. You can purchase the bagged variety, or you can create it using hot glue, or you can make it from cheesecloth or gauze. Both are inexpensive and indispensible in the number of ways they can be used. From costumes to cobwebs, you can drape it, shred it, wrap it, and hang it. It is reusable from year to year. If you do 10 yards this year, you may find yourself adding 10 more yards every year after. As the more you have, the more you can find things to do with it. The loosely woven cloth can be left white for a cleaner look or dyed for a wonderful aged look. No two dye batches will look alike and this only adds to the effect. Pile on as many layers as you can for a spooky, decrepit, webbed look that must have taken years to achieve, then let the haunting begin!

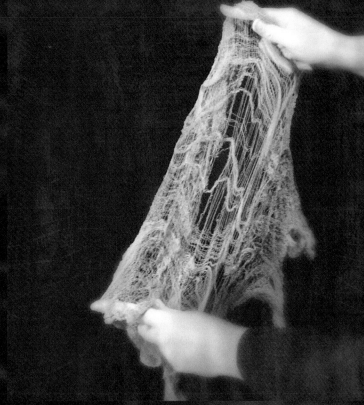

1 For an aged look, use a black, fabric dye for your cloth. Follow the manufacture's instructions for how to dye. Depending on how long you leave the cloth in the dye, and how strong the solution, you can achieve results from light gray to black.

2 Once dry, cut your cloth into approximately five foot lengths. Doing one piece at a time, stretch and pull the weave until you have what looks like a sheet of disarrayed spider stands. Don't be afraid to pull large holes into a few areas.

3 One tip to make this job easier is to put 2 small nails or screws into the top of a door frame, one on the right and one on the left. Leave the nails sticking partly out. Loop the one end of the cut cloth onto each of the nails so that it holds it into

place. Now you can do the pulling and stretching on the rest of the cloth while the cloth is suspended in the door frame instead of holding it. Tip 2: If you are doing a lot of webbing, put Band-Aids on finger parts which do the most pulling, this will keep the threads from blistering fingers.

4 Cut the ends of the cloth into tattered pieces for a finishing touch.

Hang your cloth webs as curtains or backdrops –

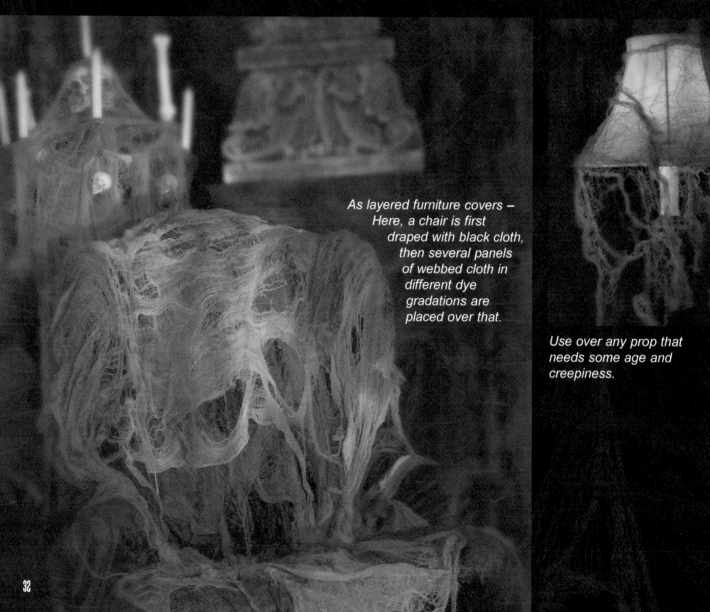

As layered furniture covers – Here, a chair is first draped with black cloth, then several panels of webbed cloth in different dye gradations are placed over that.

Use over any prop that needs some age and creepiness.

Over candle holders –

Used as layers over a costume –

Haunt Tips

Cheesecloth and gauze spiderwebbing can also be used outdoors. Use to decorate an entryway or hang down from a garden arch. The long, worn panels moving in a breeze are will cast a haunting spell.

Quickly transform a store-bought costume by safety pinning pieces of webbing cloth in random areas. Then spray the costume with Blacklight hairspray. The spray highlights all the individual strands. Once the wearer enters the Blacklight zone... everyone is bound to notice!

The more layers, the better!

Quick & Dirty Sand Casting

For A Realistic Cast-Iron Look

I f you need a quick and easy way to cast small objects for use in the haunted house, this method of sand casting is just what you need. Hot glue is used to fill the sand impressions and it's grainy, imperfect surface texture will resemble cast-iron when painted black. Keep in mind that you will only be casting a side of your object, not the entire three dimensional surface. You should be able to press the object into the sand and pull it back out.

A cemetery fence pole topper is being cast here from a metal object. To start, fill a large enough container to cast your piece which is at least 2 inches deep. The sand should be slightly moist, but not wet. Use a spray bottle to mist the sand if it dries out.

You will need: 2 or more bags of hot glue sticks, hot glue gun, craft paint or spray paint for finishing, 1 bag of paver sand, large enough container for casting object/s, spray bottle with water, casting object, spoon handle, chopsticks and pot for hot glue melting (*optional, see pages 36-37*).

Firmly press your object into the sand. Press the object in as far as possible, but not so deep that the sand covers the object. If needed, create the one inch long 'stem' that will later slip into a fence post. A spoon handle end works well here.

Gently wiggle the object from side to side to pack the sand on the sides. Very carefully lift the object straight out. You can use your finger to pat any fallen sand back into place.

Some castings with lots of detail work best being filled by a glue gun. If you are interrupted or need to take a break you can always resume filling more hot glue on top of already dried glue.

Use a cut-to-length chop-stick on back of hot glue for added support as on page 36, #4.

Hot glue is *HOT!* Do not let it touch any skin or delicate materials. A good safety tip is to keep a bowl of water with ice cubes nearby in case you get hot glue on your skin. Immediately dip the skin in the ice water to instantly cool the glue. Let casting cool completely.

Once removed from sand, brush any loose sand away. Make sure the casting is dry, then spray paint black.

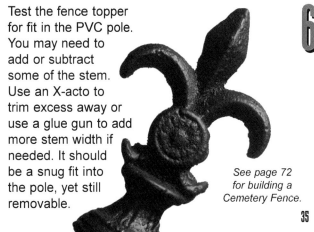

Test the fence topper for fit in the PVC pole. You may need to add or subtract some of the stem. Use an X-acto to trim excess away or use a glue gun to add more stem width if needed. It should be a snug fit into the pole, yet still removable.

See page 72 for building a Cemetery Fence.

More Examples of Cast Fence Toppers

You will need: 2 or more bags of hot glue sticks, hot glue gun, craft paint or spray paint for finishing as desired, 1 bag of paver sand, large enough container for casting object/s, 2 wooden chopsticks, 1 piece of tin foil, spray bottle of water, pot for hot glue melting (optional)

Need a safe, flexible spike to use as a fence topper? This hot glue casting is made from recycled chop sticks and tin foil. This method would also make for creative horns, finger bones or creature claws!

1 Using some tin foil and two wooden chopsticks, wrap the tin foil around one of the wooden chopsticks into a rough spike shape. Shape a pole stem on the end at least 1 inch long.

2 The sand should be slightly moist, but not wet. Use a spray bottle to mist the sand if it dries out. Press the object into the sand and wiggle slightly to firm up the sides, and then gently remove.

3 Fill the impression with hot glue using a hot glue gun.

4 While the glue is drying, carefully place the 2nd chop stick into the center of the hot glue.

5 Add some extra glue to hold the stick into place. When cool, remove the casting and spray paint black.

Step-by-step pieces from beginning to end are shown on right.

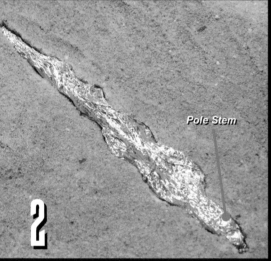

Pole Stem

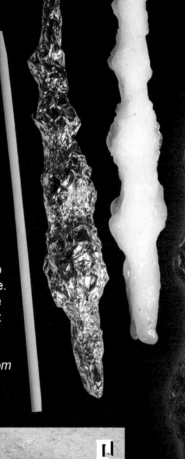

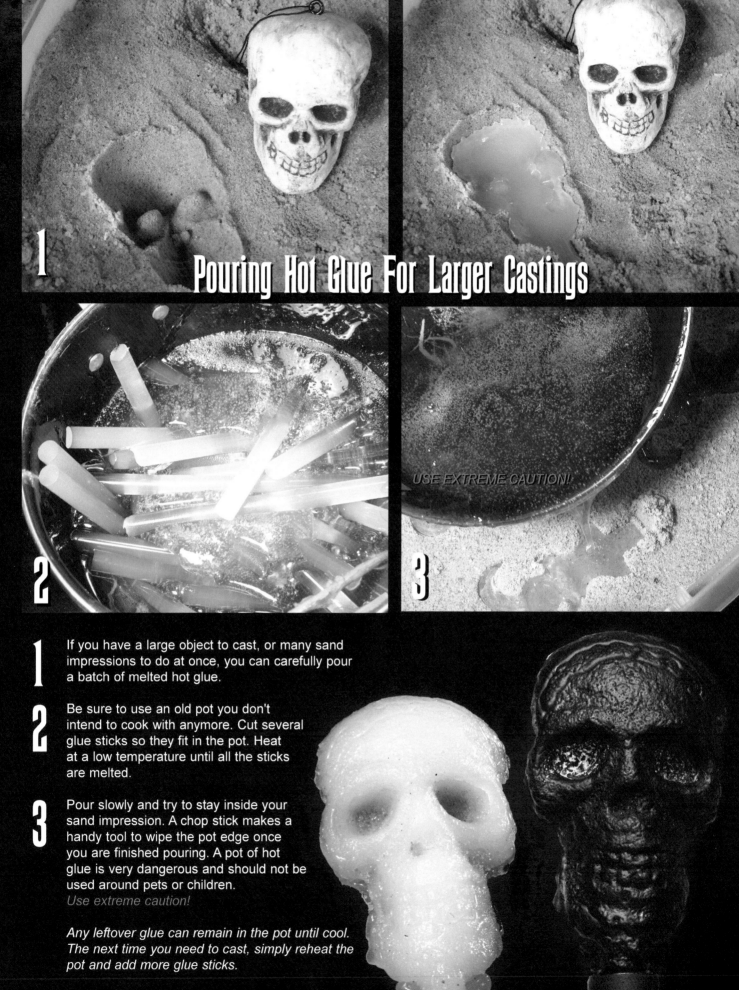

Pouring Hot Glue For Larger Castings

USE EXTREME CAUTION!

1 If you have a large object to cast, or many sand impressions to do at once, you can carefully pour a batch of melted hot glue.

2 Be sure to use an old pot you don't intend to cook with anymore. Cut several glue sticks so they fit in the pot. Heat at a low temperature until all the sticks are melted.

3 Pour slowly and try to stay inside your sand impression. A chop stick makes a handy tool to wipe the pot edge once you are finished pouring. A pot of hot glue is very dangerous and should not be used around pets or children. *Use extreme caution!*

Any leftover glue can remain in the pot until cool. The next time you need to cast, simply reheat the pot and add more glue sticks.

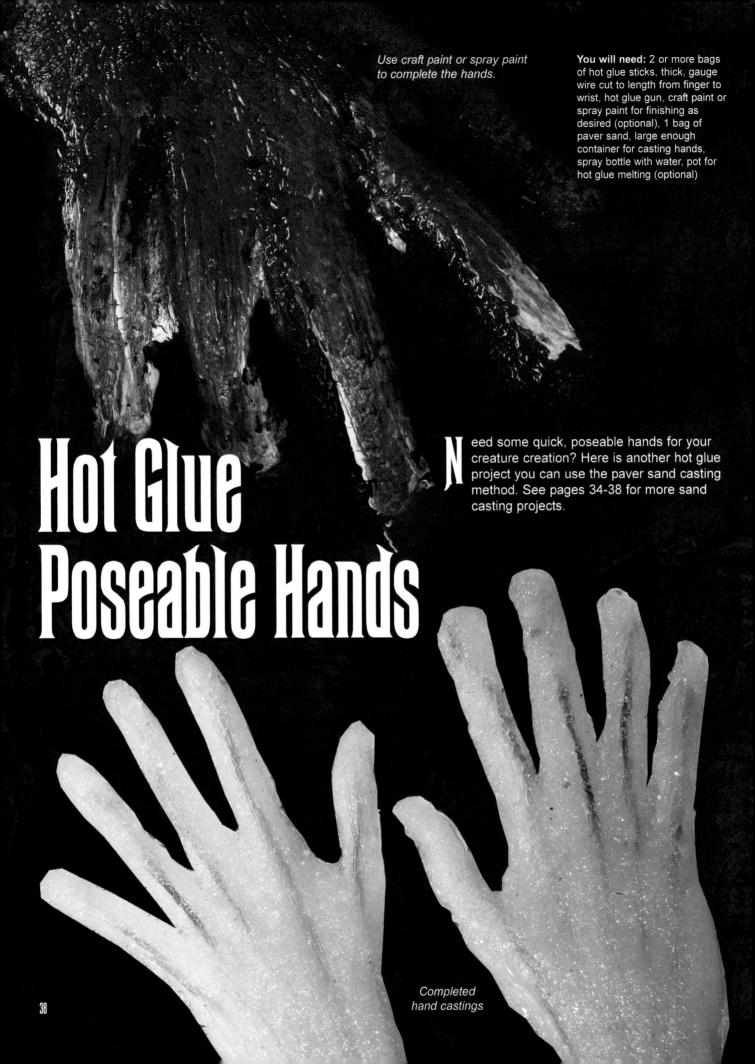

Use craft paint or spray paint to complete the hands.

You will need: 2 or more bags of hot glue sticks, thick, gauge wire cut to length from finger to wrist, hot glue gun, craft paint or spray paint for finishing as desired (optional), 1 bag of paver sand, large enough container for casting hands, spray bottle with water, pot for hot glue melting (optional)

Hot Glue Poseable Hands

Need some quick, poseable hands for your creature creation? Here is another hot glue project you can use the paver sand casting method. See pages 34-38 for more sand casting projects.

Completed hand castings

1

Using a large container filled with at least 2 inches of slightly moistened paver sand, press your hand, palm side up, into the sand firmly. Wiggle back and forth to create a compact sand impression and carefully lift the hand out.

2

You may need to use your finger to create a deeper imprint at the end of the wrist area. Do a hand imprint for both the right and left hand.

3

A hot glue gun was used to initially fill the imprint. This will help keep the imprint from collapsing when pouring melted hot glue.

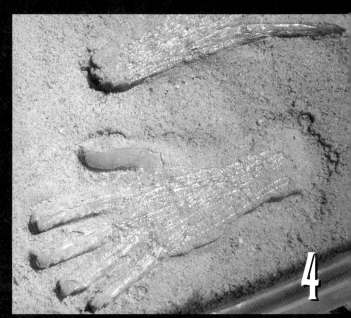

4

Shows the first layer of hot glue applied with a glue gun.

5

Carefully pour melted hot glue into the hand imprints. See page 37 for melting hot glue in a pot. *Use extreme caution!*

6

While the glue is still hot, place in wires starting at tip of each finger. Use the hot glue gun to add extra glue to cover the wires and to hold them in place.

Let cool.
Remove from sand.

Dripping Candles

L ight up your haunted house with these re-usable, safe candles. These candles look as if they have been burning all night, dripping faux, waxy trails down the sides and pooling at the candle base. Add candle holders, candelabras or just leave free-standing in a variety of shapes and sizes. As an added bonus... these hot glue candles glow-in-the-dark when used with a blacklight!

Grouping of different size candles, or candles placed at different heights using a mis-matched series of candle holders are a great look for the haunted house or graveyard.

You will need: straight PVC pipe connection pieces in various sizes or a PVC tube that has been cut into various sizes, X-acto knife, flickering tea lights, 2 or more bags of hot glue sticks, 2 inch thick Styrofoam pieces cutout to fit into the PVC pieces, bowl of ice cubes, marker, wax paper, candle stands (optional)

Place wax paper underneath before starting, as the hot glue does not stick to the wax paper.

*Remove tealight **before** adding hot glue.*

1 Firmly press the PVC piece into a sheet of Styrofoam to make an impression. Use a serrated knife to cut out the circle. Next, position a tea light in the center and trace around edge with a marker. Use an X-acto to cut out the space, without going all the way through, so that the tealight can sit inside.

2 Press the Styrofoam piece into the PVC candle. Place a sheet of wax paper under the candle. Begin applying hot glue to the candle top and sides mimicking the way a real melted candle would look.

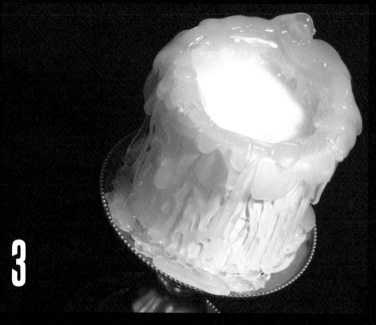

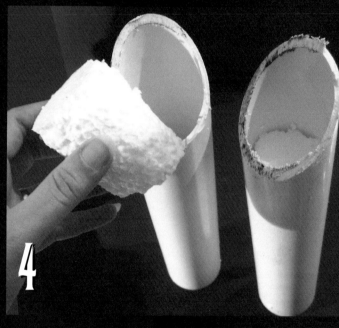

3 Build up the top, melted edge. Let the glue cool in between layers to help build height.

4 Sample of PVC pipe that has been cut on an angle for the top candle ends.

5 One way to help build height is to hold the freshly glued PVC upside down over a bowl of ice. Keep PVC moving so the glue does not run off the PVC.

6 For the bottom edge of candles without candle holders, let the hot glue pool at the base. Place wax paper underneath before starting, as the hot glue does not stick to the wax paper, it will be easy to remove. The tea lights should remain removable for easy access to turn on and change the batteries when needed.

TV and DVD Player are hidden on the right (not shown). Foreground tombstone hides Plexiglass edge. Background tombstone is behind Plexiglass and is used as a backdrop for the reflected ghost.

This effect can be used indoors or out. Take care to protect all electrical equipment from moisture, weather or breakage.

Plexiglass held up with stakes

Tombstone

Tombstone

Hidden light pointed at backdrop

Tombstone hides TV and DVD player

Viewers kept at a distance from the effect. Dotted line shows optimum viewing angle.

You will need: a TV (an old one, if using it outside), a DVD player, a sheet of Plexiglass large enough to reflect the TV image, stakes to hold up the glass, props or scene behind the glass and a light for the scene.

Pepper's Ghost
Using A TV For This Special Effect

W ho wouldn't like to see a ghost in a haunted house or cemetery on Halloween? Using an old theater trick, called the Pepper's Ghost, your viewers will feel as if they have seen a ghost. This illusion is limited to the size of the TV used so the ghost should be small in size. The advantage of using the TV version of the Pepper's ghost is movement and action. Your ghost can seem to rise up out of the ground. It can talk or appear and disappear from view. The ghost clip itself can be home-made or purchased online from various Halloween shops.

Creating The Ghost Video

This 15 second *Boney* video was shot using a video camera mounted to a tripod, a toy prop, and a black, fabric background. From behind a kitchen island, which was also covered in black fabric, the hand-held, toy prop was animated by simply raising him up, as if coming out of the ground, moving him so he seemed to look around, then having him go back down into the "ground". Only the bottom, "ground" frame should be cut off. All other parts should stay within the video frame area. The hand holding him, was covered in black fabric also.

A video editing program was used to add additional contrast. The whites were brightened, the blacks were darkened. The footage was turned into a black and white video. Videos don't have to be cinema perfect. Blurry or grainy will work just fine. It is only a reflection that will be used in the end. After the video figure disappears, several seconds of black footage was left at the end. This creates a pause before the "ghost" reappears on the final video. The completed video was then added to a DVD disk that would loop when played. *Visit the website on page 96 to download this Pepper's Ghost video clip.*

Set-up

Place a TV so it faces away from your audience. Hide the back of the TV with other props, such as tombstones or some other structure. Place a piece of Plexiglass off to one side of the TV and at an angle to the TV face. Connect the DVD player to the TV. While playing the disk, adjust the TV contrast so that the background of the video drops out as much as possible. Stand in place where your audience will be viewing the ghost.   Re-adjust the position the TV and Plexiglass, as needed, to see the reflected ghost. Set up a scene behind the glass so the ghost's transparency will be more obvious. Position a light so it illuminates the scene, but not the glass. The viewer should be able to look into the glass and see through the ghost to the scene beyond.

The Prop

The Video Camera

Boney appears to rise up out of the ground, looks around, then descends back into his grave.

The Video

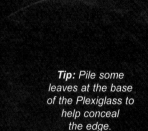

Tip: Pile some leaves at the base of the Plexiglass to help conceal the edge.

Set-up Outdoors

Shows TV with top edge draped in fabric to reduce glare and DVD Player.

Plexiglass

REST IN PEACE

Rest in Peace tombstone backdrop and *Plexiglass* set at an angle to TV.

Hidden TV

The audience's view of setup. Notice shipwheel tombstone hides left side of glass.

43

Bringing A Ghost to Life
Pepper's Ghost Using A Prop

You will need: a standing or suspended figure prop with white details that show up in blacklight, a sheet of Plexiglass large enough to reflect the prop, some black material or black plastic for a backdrop, a blacklight, a second light source (does not have to be a blacklight), props or scene placed behind the glass, some cord to suspend the prop, a ceiling hook

This version of a Pepper's Ghost can be used indoors or out. Position the prop in front of a black background. Place one or more blacklights to the side or bottom of the prop so they do not have a reflection in the glass. The glass should be at a 45 degree angle to the prop and placed so the viewers can look into the glass and see the reflected prop. Other props or structures should conceal the prop and the blacklight. Behind the glass place more props or a scene setup for the "ghost" to appear in front of. A second light source should be positioned to light the scene, but not shine on the glass itself. Use a fence or obstacle to keep the viewers at a distance to the glass and keep the hidden prop out of sight.

In the Cemetery

Suspended prop is hidden behind a large prop. Put black fabric or black plastic behind the prop and on the sides if needed. Point some blacklights at the prop, but positioned so they don't show in the glass. Position the sheet of glass so it is at a 45 degree angle to the prop, either right or left of the prop. Use stakes in front and behind the edges of the glass to hold it up. Use other strategically placed props or tree branches to conceal the stakes. You should be able to see the reflected prop in the center of the glass if standing in the viewer's position (usually behind a fence or obstruction). The goal is to control the angle the viewer will see the effect and how far away they will be from the glass.

Tip: It is dangerous to use real glass in a Pepper's Ghost effect. Someone could walk into it or break it. Plexiglass works just fine. Make sure you have a secure way of supporting it. Keep in mind that the wind may blow against it and could knock it down. Make sturdy supports wherever possible.

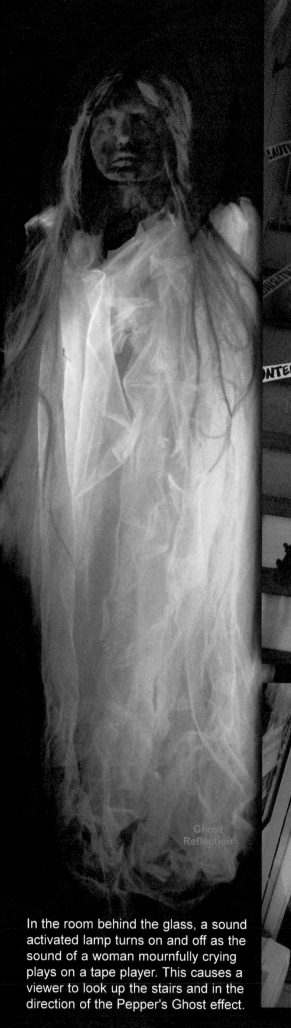

Ghost Reflection

In the room behind the glass, a sound activated lamp turns on and off as the sound of a woman mournfully crying plays on a tape player. This causes a viewer to look up the stairs and in the direction of the Pepper's Ghost effect.

Glass on angle

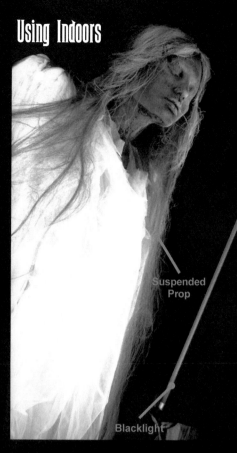

Suspended Prop

Blacklight

Shown here: Stairs are cordoned off with haunt warning tape. A door-sized piece of plexiglass is placed on an angle at the top of the stairs in a doorway. Prop is suspended from the ceiling in a small alcove at the top of the stairs to the right. A blacklight is positioned on both sides of the prop, concealed from reflection with more black cloth suspended from the ceiling.

Blacklight

They Are Watching You...

Pepper's Ghost Using A Printed Image

You will need: a printed ghost sign (*see pages 48-49*), Plexiglas (large enough to reflect image), one or more blacklights, stakes, poles, spotlights, props for back-ground scene, large structure or props to conceal ghost image, tree branches, plants, vines or faux hanging moss

Basic Setup

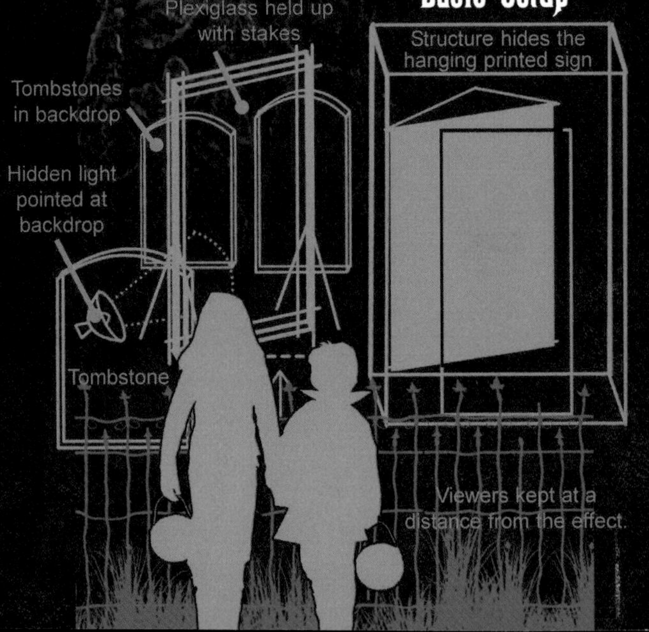

Plexiglass held up with stakes

Structure hides the hanging printed sign

Tombstones in backdrop

Hidden light pointed at backdrop

Tombstone

Viewers kept at a distance from the effect.

E ver get the feeling you are being watched? The hairs will stand up on the back of your head. Your hands will get sweaty. You look around nervously until you catch of glimpse of who is watching... when you see those eyes! Ghostly figures of the past are watching you, wanting to join in on your Halloween fun.

In the Cemetery

For Vinyl Printed Signs
See page 49

In outdoor setups the Plexiglas edges are concealed with plants, vines, and moss, hung from tree branches. If you don't have a tree in the spot you need it, duct tape branches to a pole staked into the ground. Place the tree-pole in front of the glass edge.

See pages 48-49, for a step-by-step, on how to create your own ghost image from a photo. Once printed, hang the image so it reflects in a piece of Plexiglass similar to the previous Pepper's Ghost chapters using a reflected prop or TV. Use blacklights to cause the white parts of the sign to glow and be reflected in the Plexiglass. The illuminated scene behind the glass will reveal the transparent aspect of this ghost effect.

printed sign

tree branch taped to pole and draped with faux moss

stake

scene light

Framed Plexiglas

hidden blacklight

REST IN PEACE

This Plexiglas is from a black, poster frame with backing removed.

Paper printed boy ghost

Plexiglas is barely visible even in the daylight against the background.

The one thing that every haunted house and cemetery needs– are ghosts! And plenty of them.

Indoors

This little, ghost girl appears indoors, at the top of the stairs, as on page 44 using a reflected prop. She has been printed on sheets of paper and taped together, then attached to black, foamcore board. The glass is angled in the door frame and the room behind her, dimly lit.

47

From Photo to Pepper's Ghost FX

1

I f you're not willing to lug around a TV (*page 42*) or lack the space to hide a prop for a Pepper's Ghost effect (*page 44*) there is another option. Images printed on paper or sign material make an easy to use and store Pepper's Ghost effect. To begin, you will need a photo and a few photo adjustments depending on which print version you use.

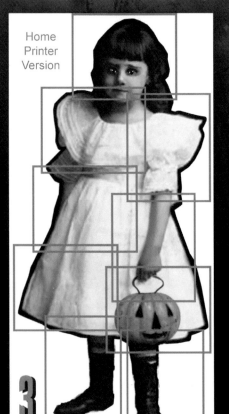

2

Home Printer Version

3 *-Home Printer Version-* Once your photo has been prepared, as in steps 1 and 2 under Photo Adjustment Steps, remove any background from the image. Create a black outline around entire figure, but leave the rest of the background white (this will save on printer ink). Enlarge image to a realistic size, depending on the size of the figure used. This sample is enlarged to 2 foot wide x 4 foot high. Divide the image into 8 x 10 inch over-lapping pieces and copy to separate files.

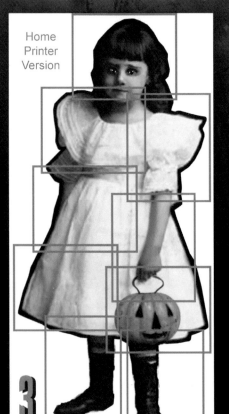

Home Printer Version

3

4 Print on regular copy paper. Trim off any unprinted margins. Tape the pieces together and cut out figure along black outline edge. Attach this to a piece of black foam core or a black painted board, as shown on right. *Note* that this version is not waterproof.

White fabric netting has been attached to board as bow.

Vinyl Sign Printed Version

Tip: Take photos of your own kids in costume to use as your home haunt *ghost*.

For an extra special effect, cut out parts like the pumpkin eyes, nose & mouth parts, and set a black box behind area with a battery operated flicker candle inside.

3

4

Vinyl Sign Printed Version

For a more permanent and weatherproof method, have the ghost image printed on vinyl banner material from a professional sign company.

3 *-Vinyl Sign Printed Version-* Adjust the ghost image using steps 1-2 as in Photo Adjustment Steps. Leave your image background black instead of white. Enlarge image to size needed and to the vinyl banner dimensions required. Follow any instructions provided by the sign company for file preparation. Request vinyl rod pockets when submitting the file to the sign printer.

4 Once the vinyl sign is done. Spray paint the ends of two pieces of PVC that are cut slightly wider than the vinyl.

5 Insert the PVC in the top and bottom into the rod pockets. Pull a string through the top PVC. Use the string to hang the vinyl sign.

Photo Adjustment Steps

1 Find a digital image of a "ghost". Any image of a figure will do. Staring straight ahead is spookiest. Child or pet-sized is easier to work with in terms of reflective glass size. The use of period clothing will add to the effect.

2 Convert the image to black and white. Add any extra elements, such as a Jack-a-lantern candy carrier. Boost the contrast of the image. Use smoothing on the face and arms if any pixilization is showing and lighten the face highlights, if needed. The white portions of the photo are what will glow under blacklight and cast a brighter reflection in the glass. Add dark shadows to the eye areas. Draw a solid black circle for each pupil and a solid white smaller circle for the eye highlight in on each of the pupils. This does not have to be exact. Remember, only a reflection of the image will be viewed.

Making Your Own
Scarecrow

W A wide, brim hat, tattered clothes blowing in the wind, bits of straw and sticks creating jagged silhouettes around it's shapeless body…the scarecrow's job is clear. To *scare*. Those brave enough to glance upwards, must decide whether it be good, or for evil, the meaning hidden in the grave-dark eyes that follow them.

You will need: carpet glue, a roll of paper towels with no pattern textures, a store bought foam skull, paint brush, serrated knife, craft paints, 2 foot length of rope twine, 1 yard of burlap fabric, 2 lengths of wire for hat, black yarn, large eyed needle, toothpicks, plastic sheeting, 1 x 2 inch pieces of wood (two 3 foot lengths, one 6 foot length), 2 wooden squares (approximately 6 x 6 inches), wood screws, hot glue gun and glue sticks, 2 yards black fabric, thin, dried branches, string

1 Adding some extra scary layers to a purchased skull will take this scarecrow to the next level of creepiness. This project requires some extra drying time so be sure to start it early.

Making Your Own
Scarecrow

2 Cut the lower jaw from the skull to create an open mouth using a serrated knife.

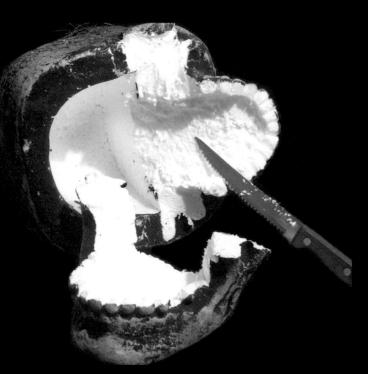

3 Use toothpicks to hold repositioned jaw in place. Hot glue the joints.

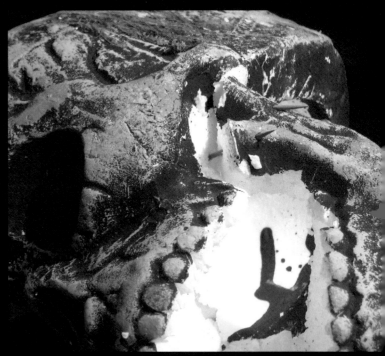

4 Cover your work area in plastic. Begin covering the skull in strips of paper towels painted with carpet glue. Roll up some strips and glue across eyes or side of jaw for a sinewy look.

5 Carpet glue is very sticky and takes a bit longer to dry. The end result has a more latex mask look and feel. Once all the layers are added, let dry completely.

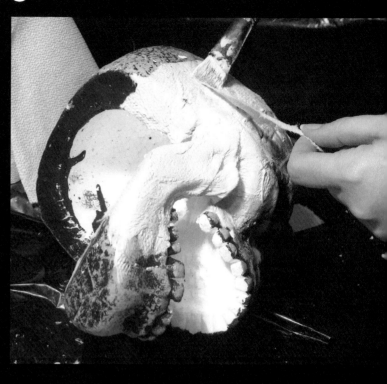

Tip: allow extra drying time when using carpet glue.

6 The completed head texture is shown above. Notice the rolled bits of paper towels across the eye and jaw that resembles sinew. Let dry completely before painting.

Making Your Own
Scarecrow

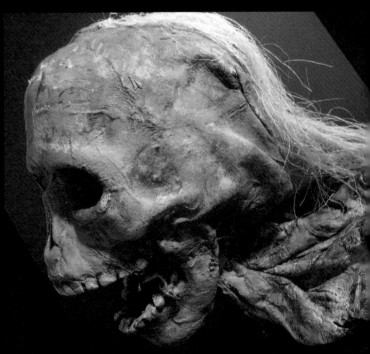

7 Paint your new head in craft paints using preferred colors. Hair is created from untwisted rope strands and hot glued in placed along the back of the head. Photo on left shows the neck formed from scrap fabric, covered with with paper towel strips and glue, then painted.

8 For the hat, form two wire circles, one smaller than the other. The smaller should fit the circumference of a head. Cover the smaller wire circle loosely with the burlap fabric. Leave enough room for a head to fit inside. Stitch with the black yarn and a large eyed needle. The stitches should be large and uneven for a haphazard appearance. Next, attach the larger circle to the burlap to create the hat rim. Turn the fabric under and stitch in place.

A spot-light pointed up from below will create some dramatic shadows.

Body Construction Diagram

Two wooden squares screwed front and back of center pole

Use two wire circles to attach fabric to.

9 The body of the scarecrow is formed from a center wood pole. At the shoulder area, use two pieces of wood as arms and angle them slightly down. Screw arms to two wooden squares to form a chest. Slip the head on top. Attach dried saplings or branches using string. Shred the ends of the black fabric and drape over the arms and back of the scarecrow for a rough coat. Tie some fabric strands to the wood arm ends to hold in place.

The Mummy
Creating A Full-figure Prop

You will need: plastic blow up figure (available from many Halloween prop shops), safety suit or old shirt and pair of pants, several rolls of duct tape, 7 yards of muslin, 4 yards of cheesecloth or gauze that has been aged (page 30), tea or coffee grounds, spray bottle, brown, black and yellow craft paints, paint brush, 2 pieces of 1x2 wood, "L" brackets, screws, pipe installation tubes, 2 heavy stones or bricks, 2 prop hands (page 38), painted, prop skull (page 50), hot glue gun, glue sticks, body stuffing (such as plastic grocery bags), Egyptian toy figures (optional), several strands of beads (optional), gold cord (optional)

Need a non-living scare-actor in your haunted setting? Why not create a life-size figure that could be used year after year. Store bought versions can be very expensive. Making your own requires a few basic materials and a little movie inspired imagination. This chapter shows a step-by-step for a mummy, but this scare-actor could be anyone or anything.

1 Tear the muslin into 3 inch strips. Soak all fabric in a pot of water and set to boil. Add tea or coffee grounds to dye fabric. Turn off heat. Let the fabric soak overnight. Drain and hang fabric strips to dry.

2 Once dyed, prepare the cheesecloth or gauze in the spider web effect (*page 30*).

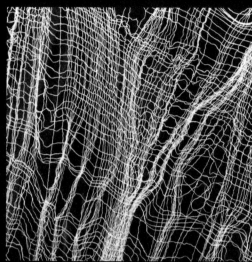

3 *Optional:* add a small amount of brown, craft paint in a spray bottle and fill with water. Spray this mixture onto the dried fabric strips for added aging effect.

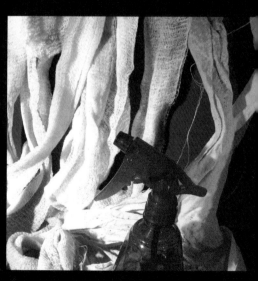

4 Cut prepared cheesecloth or gauze into 3 inch lengths and set aside.

5 Prepare head texture based on page 50 instructions.

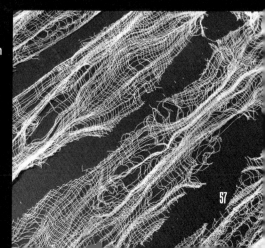

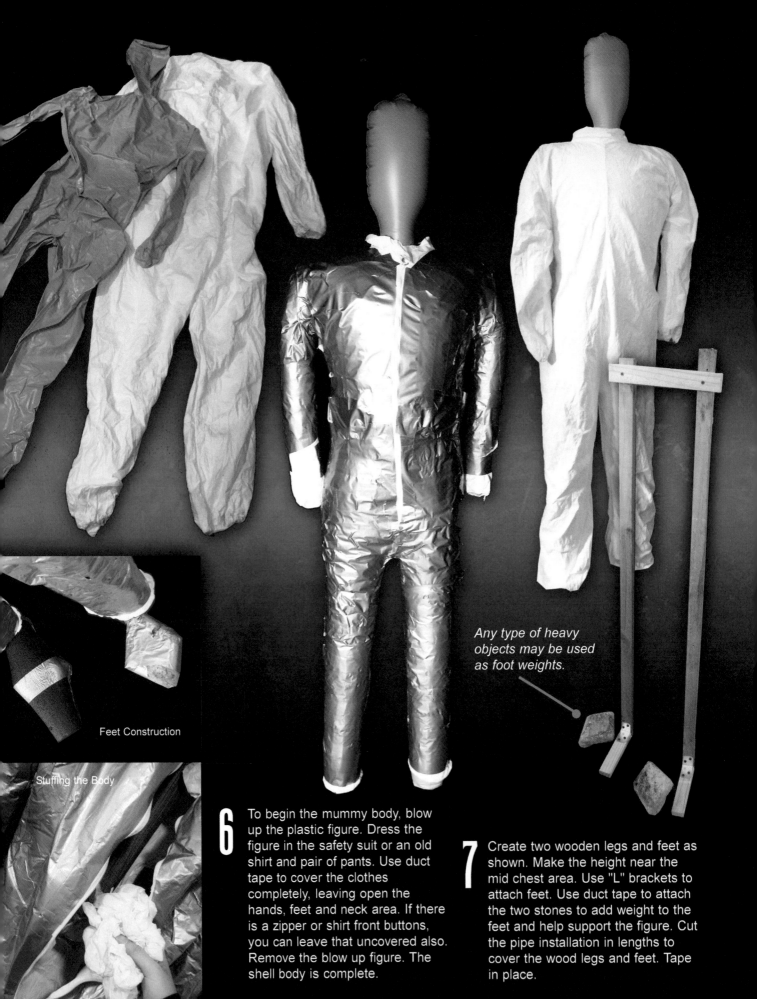

Feet Construction

Stuffing the Body

Any type of heavy
objects may be used
as foot weights.

6 To begin the mummy body, blow up the plastic figure. Dress the figure in the safety suit or an old shirt and pair of pants. Use duct tape to cover the clothes completely, leaving open the hands, feet and neck area. If there is a zipper or shirt front buttons, you can leave that uncovered also. Remove the blow up figure. The shell body is complete.

7 Create two wooden legs and feet as shown. Make the height near the mid chest area. Use "L" brackets to attach feet. Use duct tape to attach the two stones to add weight to the feet and help support the figure. Cut the pipe installation in lengths to cover the wood legs and feet. Tape in place.

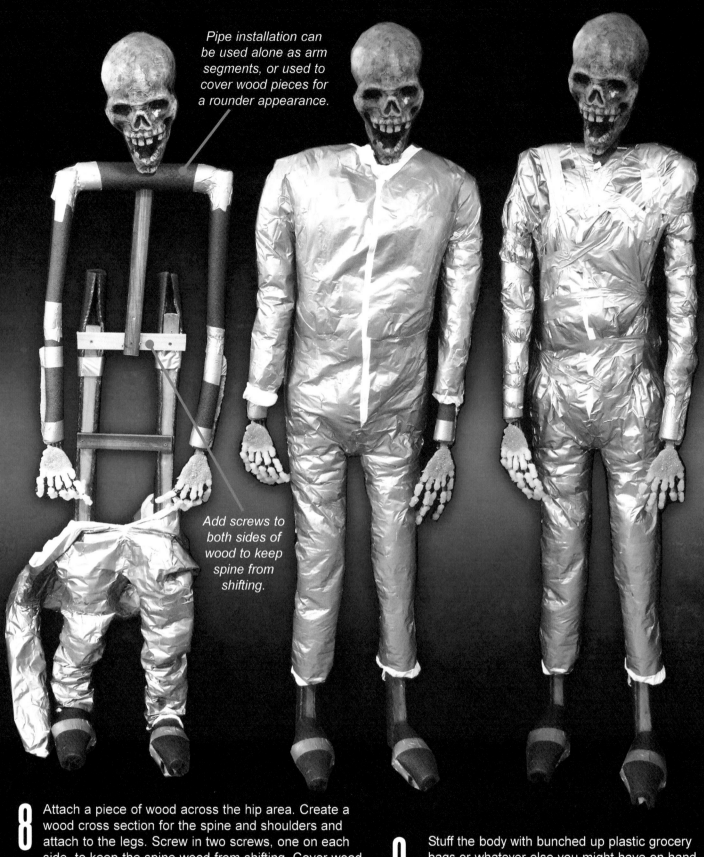

Pipe installation can be used alone as arm segments, or used to cover wood pieces for a rounder appearance.

Add screws to both sides of wood to keep spine from shifting.

8 Attach a piece of wood across the hip area. Create a wood cross section for the spine and shoulders and attach to the legs. Screw in two screws, one on each side, to keep the spine wood from shifting. Cover wood with the pipe installation and tape in place. Attach head by screwing head to neck. Arms are made from two pieces of pipe installation that have been taped in the middle. Attach prop hands to the arm ends with duct tape. Cover any exposed screw ends with extra material or wood so they do not poke through the final figure or pose a hazard when stuffing the figure. Re-dress the wooden body frame with the taped, shell body.

9 Stuff the body with bunched up plastic grocery bags or whatever else you might have on hand that would make good stuffing.

10 Once the body is stuffed, begin re-shaping the body using more duct tape. Pull in areas for a tighter, bonier appearance.

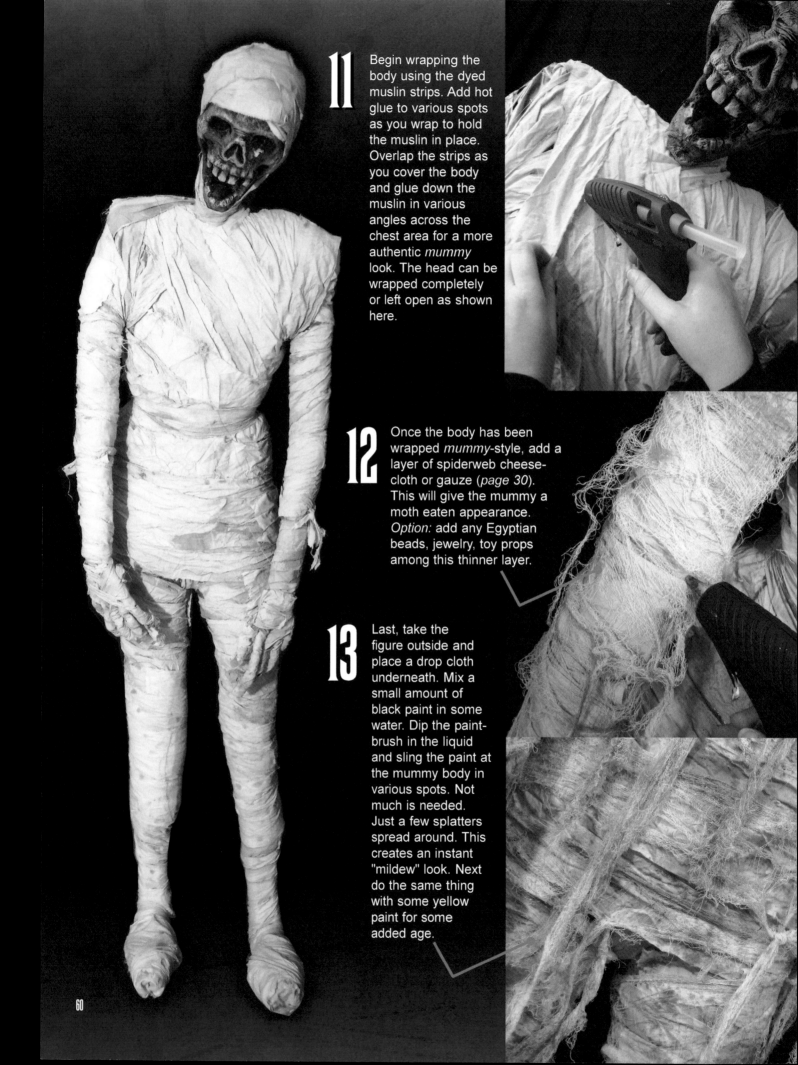

11 Begin wrapping the body using the dyed muslin strips. Add hot glue to various spots as you wrap to hold the muslin in place. Overlap the strips as you cover the body and glue down the muslin in various angles across the chest area for a more authentic *mummy* look. The head can be wrapped completely or left open as shown here.

12 Once the body has been wrapped *mummy*-style, add a layer of spiderweb cheese-cloth or gauze (*page 30*). This will give the mummy a moth eaten appearance. *Option:* add any Egyptian beads, jewelry, toy props among this thinner layer.

13 Last, take the figure outside and place a drop cloth underneath. Mix a small amount of black paint in some water. Dip the paint-brush in the liquid and sling the paint at the mummy body in various spots. Not much is needed. Just a few splatters spread around. This creates an instant "mildew" look. Next do the same thing with some yellow paint for some added age.

60

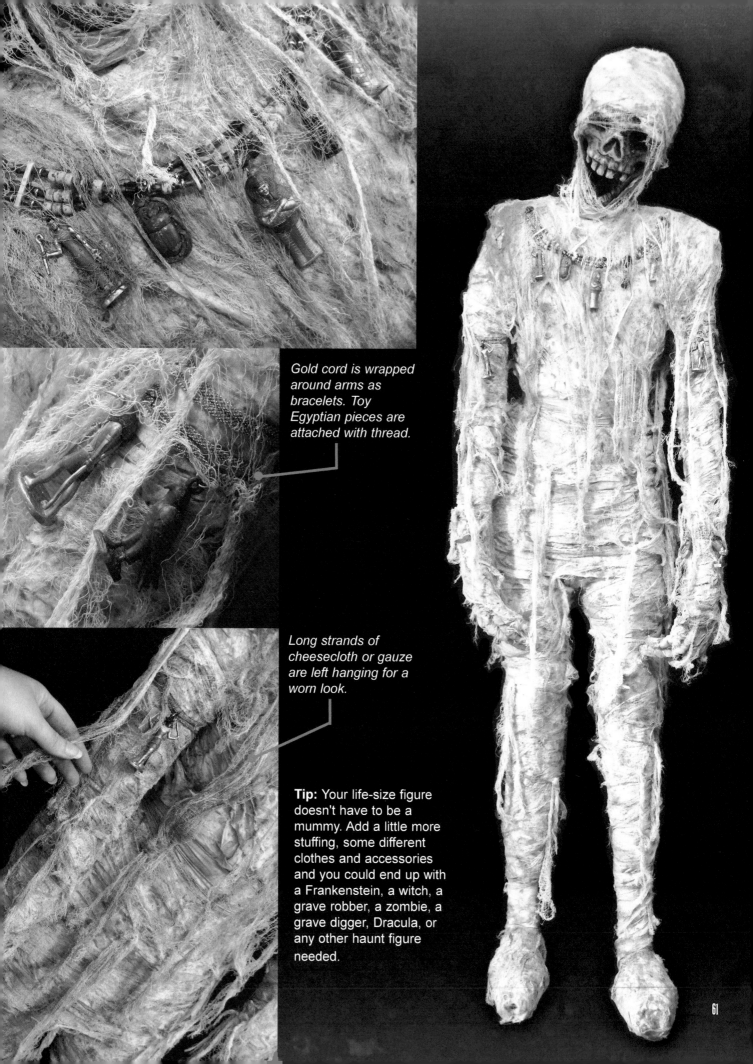

Gold cord is wrapped around arms as bracelets. Toy Egyptian pieces are attached with thread.

Long strands of cheesecloth or gauze are left hanging for a worn look.

Tip: Your life-size figure doesn't have to be a mummy. Add a little more stuffing, some different clothes and accessories and you could end up with a Frankenstein, a witch, a grave robber, a zombie, a grave digger, Dracula, or any other haunt figure needed.

The Drinking Ghoul
With an Unending Thirst

This drinking ghoul cannot satisfy its undead thirst. The liquid keeps on pouring and the ghoul keeps on drinking. He appears to have just crawled up out of a grave. This ghoul's bucket "body" is concealed by a tattered, dirty shirt. One arm reveals a skeleton bone. In a shrunken hand is the bottle it cannot put down.

You will need: one plastic bottle with long neck, a small pond pump, a bucket, a prop head (*page 50*), paper towels, carpet glue, rubber tubing, an old shirt, a prop arm bone, craft paints, hot glue gun, glue sticks, 1x2 wood pieces cut to size, wood screws, pipe installation tubing, long neck funnel, scissors, X-acto knife, duct tape, one poseable prop hand (*page 38*), "L" brackets, zip ties

Creating the ghoul tongue

Creating the ghoul neck

1 To create the ghoul's tongue use one paper towel folded into a triangle. Then fold each side in again for a diamond shape. Fold the pointed tip down and then fold the sides in once more. Open up the inside pocket and stuff with some more paper towel pieces. Mold the sides under and form a bend in the whole piece.

2 Form the head similar to page 50. Hot glue the tongue into the open month and brush with carpet glue to match head texture.

3 Cut the top end off the long neck funnel.

4 Hot glue the funnel neck to the prop head with a hot glue patch. See page 65 to find out how to create a hot glue patch. Paint the neck and patch to match the head.

5 Screw together four pieces of wood as shown. The "spine" wood should reach all the way to the ground. Duct tape the center wood piece to the bucket. Zip tie the prop neck to the wood. Place the pump in bottom of the bucket. Connect the plastic tubing to the pump all the way up to the hand area, with some excess left over.

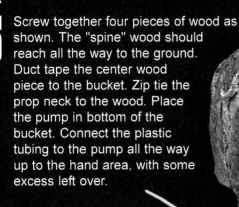

Plastic tubing zip-tied from pump and along wood to reach the hand / bottle area.

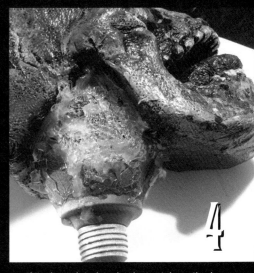

Attach neck to head using patch method shown on page 65.

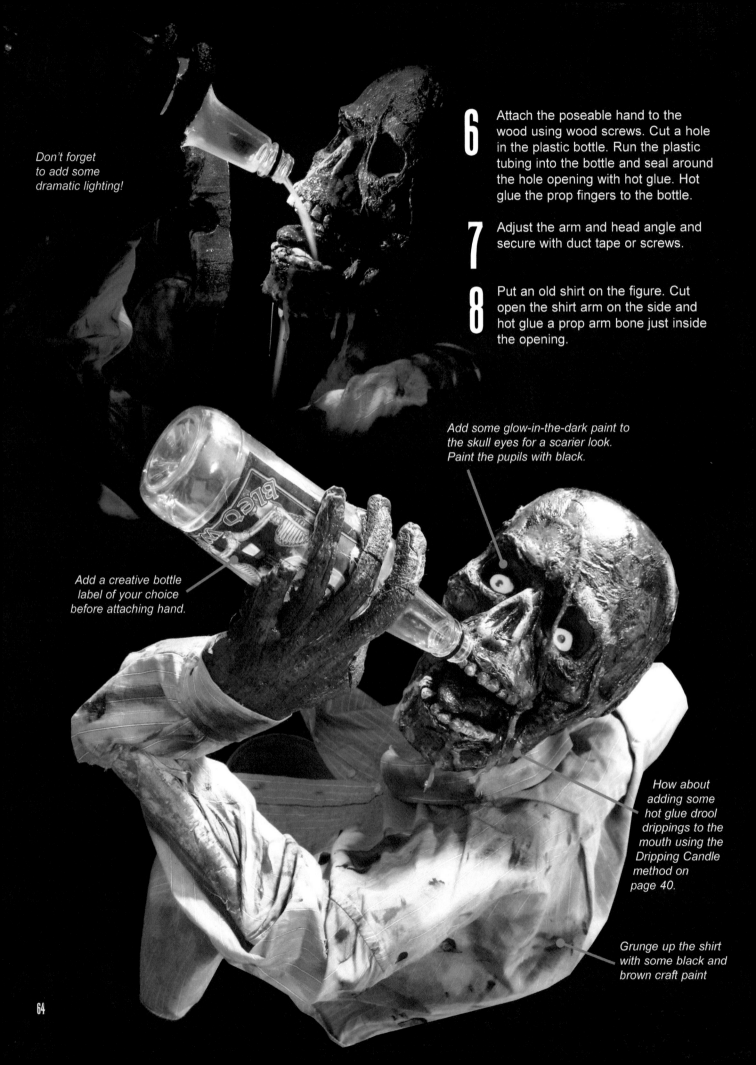

Don't forget to add some dramatic lighting!

6 Attach the poseable hand to the wood using wood screws. Cut a hole in the plastic bottle. Run the plastic tubing into the bottle and seal around the hole opening with hot glue. Hot glue the prop fingers to the bottle.

7 Adjust the arm and head angle and secure with duct tape or screws.

8 Put an old shirt on the figure. Cut open the shirt arm on the side and hot glue a prop arm bone just inside the opening.

Add some glow-in-the-dark paint to the skull eyes for a scarier look. Paint the pupils with black.

Add a creative bottle label of your choice before attaching hand.

How about adding some hot glue drool drippings to the mouth using the Dripping Candle method on page 40.

Grunge up the shirt with some black and brown craft paint

9

Shirt conceals ghoul's spine and back hump which are attached to the bucket

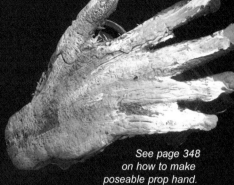

See page 348 on how to make poseable prop hand.

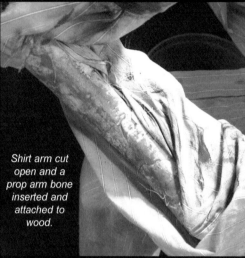

Shirt arm cut open and a prop arm bone inserted and attached to wood.

9 To help fill out the figure's back, attach a bent piece of installation tubing to the spine and duct tape in place.

10 When placing the figure in the haunt setting, open the shirt so the water will run into the bucket. Place tombstones or other props around figure to hide the bucket.

11 Fill the bucket with enough water to cover the pond pump. Turn pump on to test. Make any adjustments needed for the liquid to pour from the bottle into the mouth and from the mouth into the bucket.

Plastic tube is run up the arm along the wood and inserted into bottle.

Making a Hot Glue Patch

Use a hot glue gun and a bowl of water. Use the hot glue gun to draw a series of overlapping circles over the water. Then draw random swirls of hot glue to fill in the patch. When the glue is cool, remove from the water. This can be used to fill a large open area of hot glue on props or as an interesting texture to be applied to all sorts of other projects. Paint as needed.

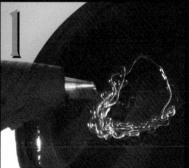

Endless Mausoleum

You will need: 1x2 wood, L brackets, wood screws, black & silver spray paint, 2 inch & 3/4 inch thick Styrofoam, 2 sheets of Plexiglass cut to the size needed, Gila Privacy Window Film, 2 pieces of metal Plexiglass railing, white house paint primer, black, latex enamel house paint, spray foam, drill, hot tool, halogen shop light or hanging plugin light, 2 pool swimming noodles, black, white, red, brown craft paints, paint brushes, two strips of Velcro, duct tape, toothpicks

Your guests will get a spine tingling chill when looking into the Endless Mausoleum of moldy crypts. Row upon row of crypt plaques will stretch into infinity through the use of mirrored surfaces, lighting and prop walls. The basic structure is a wood frame made to support the Styrofoam walls and ceiling. The front and back walls contain special effect prop glass.

1

Pre-drill holes before adding screws.

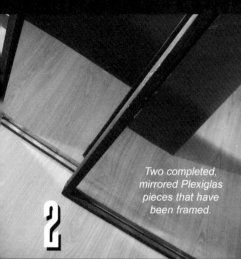

2

Two completed, mirrored Plexiglas pieces that have been framed.

3

Corner of frame

Create two dead, faux flower and moss arrangements.

Building the Inner Structure

1 Cut the metal railing pieces ¼ inch shorter than each of the Plexiglas sides for both pieces of Plexiglas. Cut the wood to match the lengths of the shorter end of both pieces of Plexiglas. For the longer sides, cut the wood 2 inches longer than the Plexiglas. Pre-drill the holes and screw the metal pieces to the centers of each wood piece. Spray paint all assembled pieces black.

2 Cover one side each for the two Plexiglas pieces with Gila Privacy Mirror Window Film. Follow the manufacturer's instructions on how to apply. On the back of one piece of Plexiglas (not the film side) spray paint with silver paint. This will be the back mirrored wall.

3 Use L brackets to attach the wood frame sections together for each Plexiglas sheet.

4 Cut 4 pieces of 1x2 wood for braces for the depth needed between the two framed pieces of Plexiglas. This depth can be whatever is needed. This sample was 3 feet deep. Stand the wood brace on its side next to the L bracket edge for both the top and the bottom and attach with a second L bracket as shown. The 2 inch thick Styrofoam wall will rest against this edge.

5 Measure the inside of the floor area between the wood pieces. Cut a piece of 2 inch thick Styrofoam to fit inside for the inner floor. Measure the side openings the same way and cut 2 inch Styrofoam walls for the right and left sides. Fit the pieces into place and trim if necessary. It should be snug, but not tight.

6 Your construction should now form a box with two Plexiglas walls for the front and back.

7 Cut 8 pieces of 1 inch thick Styrofoam rectangle wall plaques, so that two will fit across the inside side walls. Use a hot tool to create a roughened, one inch border on each plaque. Glue the plaques to the inner walls so that they are evenly spaced out, four on each side. Let dry.

Top Brace

4

Side Wall

Back Wall Reflection

Floor

5

Front Plexiglas

Completed Box Structure

6

7

Building the Parts

Raise the structure up and rest on four milk crates or build a similar wooden box as a base (*see page 69*). Use 1 inch Styrofoam to create wall base pieces for the top and bottom of each side wall. This will hide the milk crates and cover the structure's wood frame.

Create corner covers with 3/4 inch Styrofoam cut to match structure height. Duct tape the corner pieces together. Cut roof piece to cover top opening with some overhang. Create a front cap to cover the top, front edge of the structure. Use two straps of Velcro to attach to back of light on the inside of the structure. The front cap has squares attached to face with a one inch space between each. Use craft glue and toothpicks to attach.

Create pillars using 2 inch thick Styrofoam for short, pillar side walls on either side of the front opening. At the top and bottom of each pillar wall is a 2 inch thick pillar cap cut wider and longer than the wall piece. The footer cap has two stacked pieces of 2 inch Styrofoam. Use two swimming pool noodles that have been cut open to wrap around the front each of each pillar wall. Trim to fit height. Use craft glue and tooth picks to hold noodle to the wall. Use craft glue and toothpicks to attach all the pillar pieces together. Also, create a pillar to pillar top piece. Create an open box shape with five pieces of 2 inch thick Styrofoam. Add more evenly, spaced squares across the front with glue and toothpicks. This section will rest on top of the top pillar caps, not attached to the pillars.

The front step is made with three pieces of 2 inch thick Styrofoam. This piece will cover the front milk crates and the bottom Plexiglas edge. It fits snugly between the two columns. Cut notches in the sides of the step to fit over pillar foot caps. Use duct tape for the seams. Glue and toothpick joined pieces to reinforce.

Styrofoam Parts Assembled

***Monster Mud* Parts Assembled**

Velcro Front Inner Cap to back of light.

Left Outer Wall

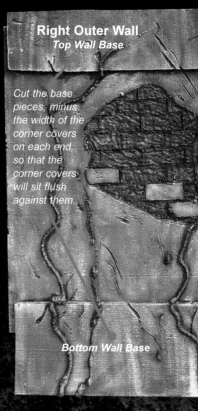

Right Outer Wall
Top Wall Base

Cut the base pieces, minus the width of the corner covers on each end, so that the corner covers will sit flush against them.

Bottom Wall Base

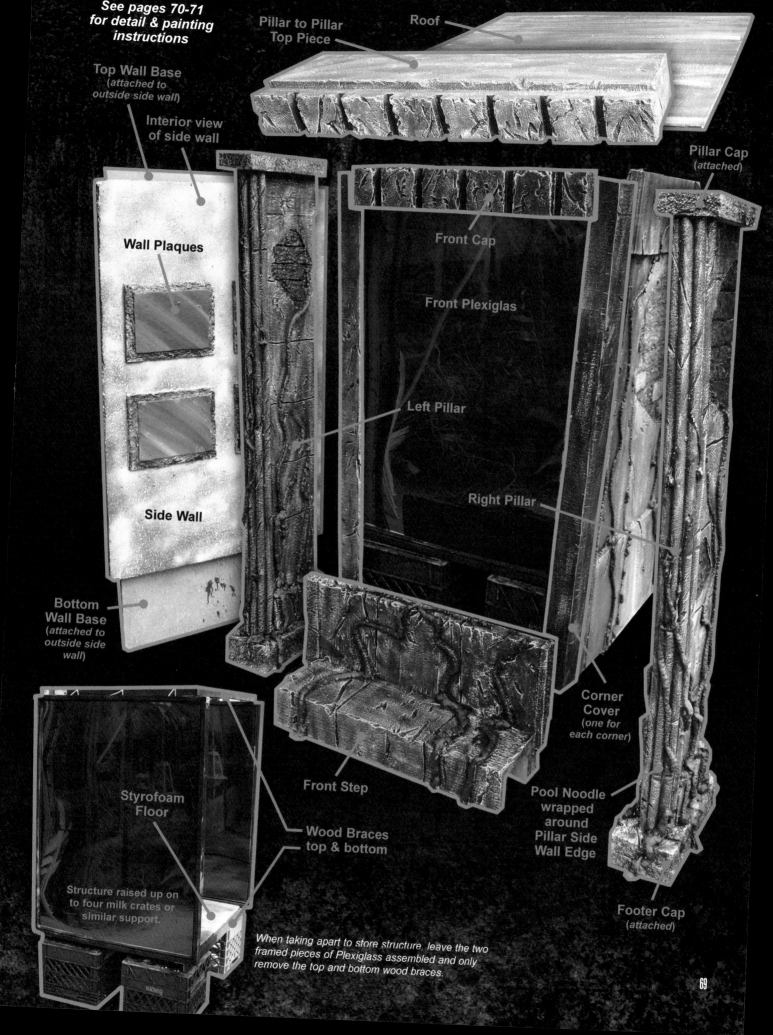

See pages 70-71 for detail & painting instructions

Top Wall Base (attached to outside side wall)

Interior view of side wall

Pillar to Pillar Top Piece

Roof

Pillar Cap (attached)

Wall Plaques

Front Cap

Front Plexiglas

Left Pillar

Side Wall

Right Pillar

Bottom Wall Base (attached to outside side wall)

Corner Cover (one for each corner)

Front Step

Pool Noodle wrapped around Pillar Side Wall Edge

Styrofoam Floor

Wood Braces top & bottom

Structure raised up on to four milk crates or similar support.

Footer Cap (attached)

When taking apart to store structure, leave the two framed pieces of Plexiglass assembled and only remove the top and bottom wood braces.

Exterior Details

Push in toothpicks at various angles to attach corner covers to walls. When disassembling structure, simply remove the toothpicks.

Creating The Details

1 Using a hot tool, carve details to outer structure, such as cracks, stone lines, bricks. Here pieces of plaster seem to have fallen away to reveal underlying brick wall. The bricks are sculpted with a rougher texture that is also slightly lower than the plaster layer. See page 68 for the completed Styrofoam structure.

2 Use spray foam to create vines on side walls, step and pillars. Do not overlap the spray foam on Styrofoam pieces that come apart. Start vine at bottom and spray in a wavy line going upwards. Let dry.

3 Remove all Styrofoam pieces from wooden structure. Prop up the wood frame when these pieces are removed so it doesn't tip over. *Monster Mud (page 13)* all pieces on all sides. Let dry. See page 68 for the completed *Monster Mud* structure.

4 Follow the painting instructions on page 71 for the interior and exterior mausoleum sections.

Lighting

For the interior light, wrap a halogen light fixture with a purple, or blue, color cellophane. This will add a color cast to the light.

Hanging light can also be used. Add another piece of wood in center and zip tie chain.

Use L brackets to screw wood pieces to the top, side braces for each light used. Attach lights with zip ties. Run the light plugs along the top and out the back to plug in.The roof will lay on top of this section and hide cords.

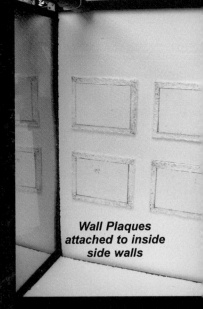

Wall Plaques attached to inside side walls

Pool Noodle wrapped around Pillar Side Wall

Hot Tool Used to carve designs into Styrofoam

Spray Foam used to create Vines

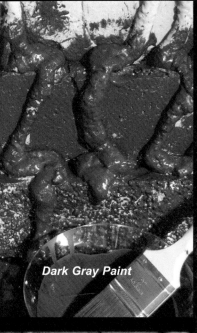

Dark Gray Paint

Black Paint

Red Paint

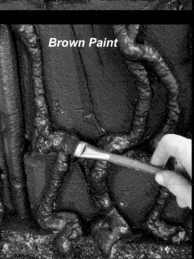

Brown Paint

Painting

Paint the interior sides (side walls, roof and floor) of the Styrofoam pieces to resemble marble using craft paints. Let dry.

For the outside portions of the Styrofoam a stickier mixture of paint is used. This helps to hold the vines, the spongy, pool noodles and Monster Mud together better. Dark gray base paint mixture: mix white, house paint primer with black, latex enamel house paint until you get a dark gray color. Use a large brush to cover all the unpainted Styrofoam.

Next, use a smaller brush to paint along all the vines, in all the nooks and crannies or cut marks with solid black craft paint.

For the brick Styrofoam portions, drag a brush with red paint over the raised brick texture to cover only the top texture edges.

Paint all the vines with brown, craft paint.

Finally, drag a dry brush with a small amount of white paint over the surface texture of the Styrofoam wall areas. This will highlight only the raised areas and really bring out the "stone" look of the pieces. Let dry.

Completed Mausoleum

Props added to the interior are reflected endlessly in the Plexiglas. In order to test the effect, look through the front while it is dark. Otherwise, lift up the roof and check the infinity reflection through the top.

White Paint

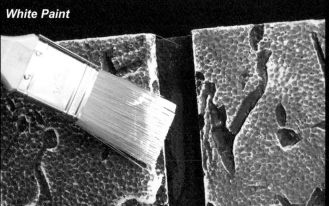

Interior Side Walls Painting

71

Graveyard Fence

You will need: two 1x2 wood pieces for each fence section, 2 wooden stakes per fence section, wood screws, drill with 7/8 drill bit, ½ inch PVC poles cut to various lengths *(PVC thickness here won't matter. The wood will keep the poles from moving around)*, PVC cutter tool, premade fence toppers (page 34), black spray paint, hammer, short pieces of rebar *(optional)*

Show your visitors the way through your yard haunt and keep them at a safe distance from your props at the same time with a cemetery fence. This fence is easy to assemble and take apart for storage later.

Vary the fence post heights for more interest.

PVC cutter or a saw may be used to cut the poles.

1 Use a 7/8 drill bit to cut equal spaced holes in both pieces of 1x2 wood. The holes need to line up for the poles to fit into.

2 Screw two L brackets to each stake. Leave at least five inches at top and bottom of each stake.

3 Attach both wood pieces to poles with screws as shown.

4 Use PVC cutters or saw to cut desired lengths for the PVC poles.

5 Spray paint the entire fence section. Let dry.

6 When setting up your fence loosen the soil at the stakes. Hammer the stakes several inches into the ground. Press the soil firmly around each stake. Make sure the fence can stand up should anyone grab hold of it. For extra support, drive rebar through the inside of the poles and at fence ends where needed.

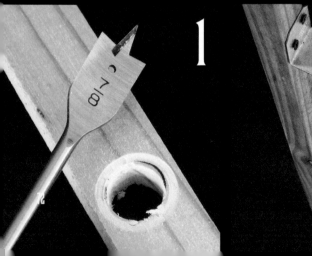

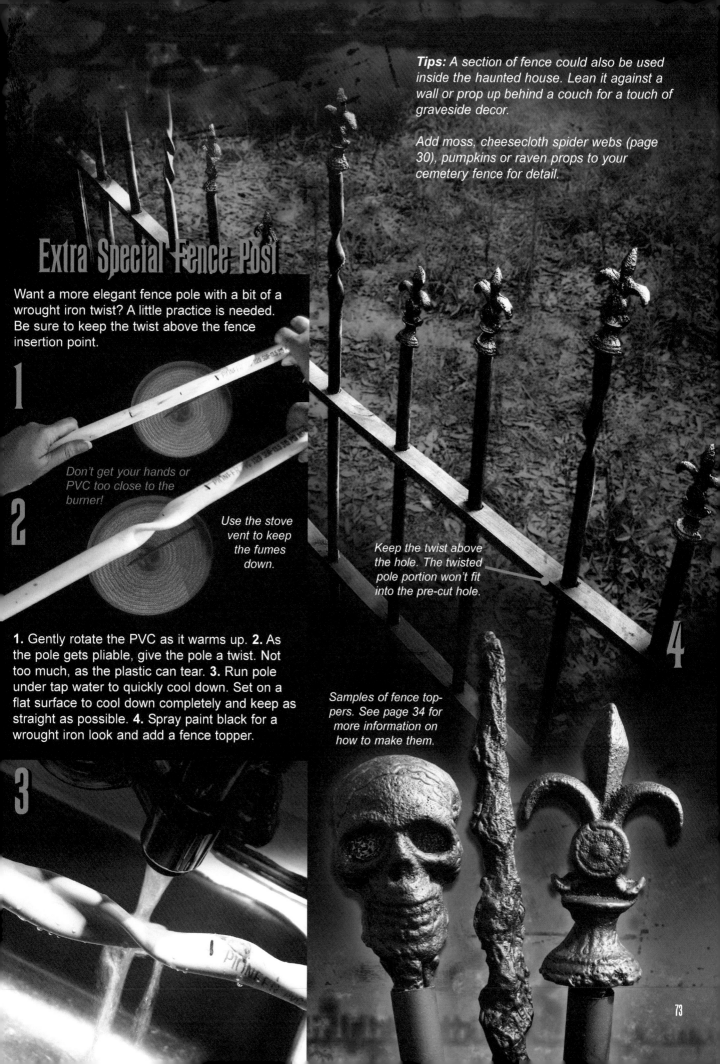

Tips: *A section of fence could also be used inside the haunted house. Lean it against a wall or prop up behind a couch for a touch of graveside decor.*

Add moss, cheesecloth spider webs (page 30), pumpkins or raven props to your cemetery fence for detail.

Extra Special Fence Post

Want a more elegant fence pole with a bit of a wrought iron twist? A little practice is needed. Be sure to keep the twist above the fence insertion point.

1

Don't get your hands or PVC too close to the burner!

2

Use the stove vent to keep the fumes down.

Keep the twist above the hole. The twisted pole portion won't fit into the pre-cut hole.

4

1. Gently rotate the PVC as it warms up. **2.** As the pole gets pliable, give the pole a twist. Not too much, as the plastic can tear. **3.** Run pole under tap water to quickly cool down. Set on a flat surface to cool down completely and keep as straight as possible. **4.** Spray paint black for a wrought iron look and add a fence topper.

Samples of fence toppers. See page 34 for more information on how to make them.

3

What To Use For
Special Effect Lighting

1 Strobe Light

2 Lamp attached to a Lighting FX box which is sound activated.

3 Black Light

4 Christmas tree lights. Blue, white, orange, and gold are all useful in the home haunt setting.

5 Battery operated tealight

1 Strobe Light
Use it for lightning or intense drama and enhanced action from *scare*actors.

2 Lighting FX
The Lighting FX box is attached to a lamp. Any sound will cause the lamp to flicker in time with the sound. Great for creating a *ghostly* presence.

3 Blacklight
Blacklights come in many shapes and sizes. Anything that contains white or glow-in-the-dark paint will glow under blacklight.

4 Christmas tree lights
White, blue, reds, orange and yellow strings of Christmas tree lights can be used in a variety of ways in the haunt setting. Use red and yellow lights for fire effect and blue and white for accent lights.

With all the props and special effects in place, it's time to light the scene. The color and type of lighting is one of personal preference. Red, blue, yellow, green, white, strobe, black-light, flicker lights and a mixture of any of these, will all work in a haunted setting. Use caution when setting up lights. Some lights can get hotter than others. Be aware of anything near lights or bulbs and follow the manufactures' instructions and warnings. Remember that Styrofoam melts with heat so don't place your hand-crafted prop too close to a hot light.

5 Battery operated Tealights
Use as is or as part of the Dripping Candles project (*page 40*). Use flickering tealights for a more realistic look.

6 Battery operated Candles
Flickering bulbs on candles or chandeliers set just the right mood for the haunted house setting.

7 Spotlights
Use spotlights to direct the lighting over larger areas outdoors. Spotlight bulbs come in white, blue, green, yellow and red.

8 LED UV Flashlight
Great for small, accent spotlight.

Spotlight
Bulbs come in white, blue, green, yellow and red

Battery operated candle

6

7

8 *LED UV Flashlight*

Fog Machine Effects

An outdoor Halloween setting just would not be complete without some eerie fog rolling among the tombstones. Properly placed in your setting, a fog machine can add instant drama. In order for it to really work at its best, the fog needs to hug the ground and move around your prop pieces. To do this, either the weather needs to be cool, or your emitted fog needs to be chilled. It's unlikely you will be able to locate a weather witch to give you the optimum outdoor temperature, but there are various methods that home haunters have come up with to chill the fog.

You will need: fog machine, plastic garbage can with lid, at least 6' of aluminum dryer hose, frozen 12 ounce drink bottles filled with water, ice, fog juice, fog machine timer, PVC pipe large enough to fit over the fog machine end and can have water bottles inserted with some free space around them, water resistant duct tape, leaves, black cloth (optional)

Having props, such as, tree branches, tombstones, Jack-a-lanterns, skeleton arms that reach out of the ground– all look extra creepy surrounded by a layer of fog.

Trash Can Chiller

One popular method of chilling fog is the trash can chiller. Attach several lengths of dryer hose together using water resistant duct tape. Cut two holes in a plastic, trash can that can fit the dryer hose in and out of. Run the hose around the inside of the trash can and loop back down through the middle and out of the second hole in the front. Use more duct tape to seal the openings around the holes. Fill the spaces around the trash can hose inside with ice and frozen bottles of water. Turn on the fog machine and set the timer right before your guests arrive. As the fog is forced into the length of hose, it will be chilled. As it comes out, it will hug the ground and provide the perfect graveyard effect!

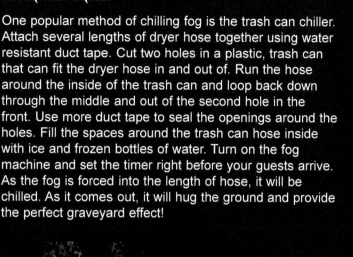

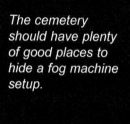

The cemetery should have plenty of good places to hide a fog machine setup.

Cover the dryer hose around the end opening with leaves or black cloth to conceal.

PVC Pipe Chiller

Place the fog machine and it's timer in the back of your outdoor setting, out of site from your viewers. Conceal the fog machine with props or tombstones. Place a PVC pipe around the fog machine opening and secure with waterproof duct tape. Make sure the whole setup is out of danger of being stepped on or tripped over. Surrounding it with a collection of tombstones is a good idea. Fill the PVC pipe with frozen, drink bottles. Cover the pipe with a black cloth and leaves to conceal. Turn on the fog machine and set the timer right before your guests arrive.

Pack the ice and bottles around the hose inside the trash can. Use duct tape to connect multiple lengths of dryer hose, if needed.

77

Making An Entrance

This store-bought prop was repainted black with white highlights. A simple wooden box was added below as a pillar and painted to match.

When your guests step up to the door, give them a taste of what is to come from the moment they cross the threshold. A collection of Jack-a-lanterns and a scarecrow and some crows, a witch and a bubbling cauldron with green lights, a couple of gargoyles on top of some stone pillars, or a collection of tombstones and a shovel sitting beside the door…any grouping of props and effects could be used at the front entrance to your haunted house. Adding details such as sound effects, FX lighting, or layers of cheesecloth spider's web blowing in the breeze are easy additions.

Guests here are greeted by two menacing gargoyles and a canopy of spider-webs. A carpet of leaves surround the mini pumpkin patch.

Setting the Stage:
Inside the Haunted House

After weeks of decorating, the house goes from everyday, to deliciously derelict and spooky. Party-goers will have as much fun conversing with their fellow tricksters and eating the festive fall food, as they will strolling through the halls of gray and gloom! It's the one time of the year when letting a little house dirt go will work in your favor and add to the atmosphere. Lighting, scents, gauzy textures on every surface...your guests' senses will awaken to a darker side of fun.

Inexpensive, purchased props can be combined for a more interesting effect. Here, a raven statue is wrapped in faux barbwire.

Use plug-in pumpkins inside. Use a multi-plug outlet and group them at the base of a table or along the back of a couch.

MITCHELL 2007

This maid will gladly take your hat... and your head. The Butler is ready with some finger food... literally.

MITCHELL 2007

82

Make imaginative groupings of props. It can be funny, macabre, scary... and don't forget the bugs, spiders, frogs and snakes!

Purchase faux Spanish moss and hang it from ceilings, over mausoleums, around the buffet, or in doorways. Add layers of cheesecloth spider webbing too!

Use wrinkled, white sheets over furniture for an abandoned house look.

There are many directions a haunted house theme can take. Some are made for horror, with lots of blood, sharp instruments and body parts. Others are more about atmosphere and suspense. And some may seem homey, yet slightly decrepit and abandoned sort of haunted house...where one might imagine ghosts wandering the dark halls at night and the echoing sounds of footsteps when no one is there. Whatever your home haunt preference-be sure to add the details that will convey the story your house has to tell. From the moment your visitors arrive to the moment they leave, make a statement. Plan out how your guests will move through the space and what will they see. Let your creativity spark their imaginations...and your guests will be leave thinking... *I wonder what next year will hold?*

Pile on the rats, the bats, the ravens and skulls...

Every nook and cranny of the haunted house becomes a theater of the eerie and the macabre.

1809-1849
Edgar Allan Poe

And my soul from out
that shadow
that lies floating
on the floor
Shall be lifted

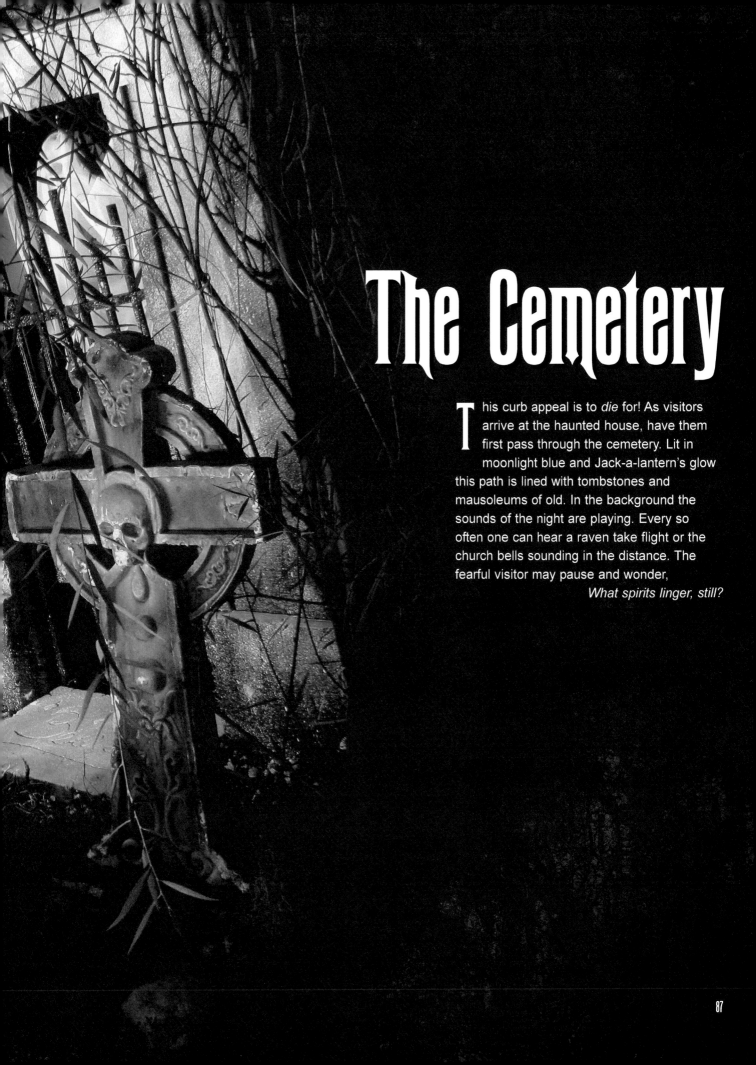

The Cemetery

This curb appeal is to *die* for! As visitors arrive at the haunted house, have them first pass through the cemetery. Lit in moonlight blue and Jack-a-lantern's glow this path is lined with tombstones and mausoleums of old. In the background the sounds of the night are playing. Every so often one can hear a raven take flight or the church bells sounding in the distance. The fearful visitor may pause and wonder,

What spirits linger, still?

Don't be afraid to inject a little Halloween humor into the scene.

Save up a bag or two of dry leaves to spread out at the front door. The crunching under foot will add to the spooky atmosphere.

We love our fear of the unknown. We like mysterious, cold spots and things that make us jump. We smile at being caught off guard and laugh often when something makes our hair stand on end. We are at home with ghosts, and spooks, and creaky doors. It's Halloween again– our favorite time of the year. Time to embrace our fear of the dark and things that go bump in the night!

Top an old, plaster pillar with a store bought prop and wrap them with strands of moss.

Daylight can bring chills too—
with all the more details to see.

Let the lawn work go—
props look right at home
in overgrown grass and
untrimmed trees.

Halloween can bring smiles
as well as screams!

Halloween is great for the imagination. Ordinary can extraordinary! Recycle and re-craft or dare to create something new.

Here, an ordinary birdbath can suddenly become a fire pit for the witch's cauldron.

Other Resources

http://www.halloween-l.com Online gathering place for home haunt enthusiasts. View tutorials,photos, videos and more.

http://halloweenpropmaster.com/ Great resource for home haunt DVDs and tutorials.

http://hauntspace.com/ A forum for home haunters and haunted attraction enthusiasts.

http://www.homehauntersassociation.com Provides home haunters with a place to register their home haunt, advertise, meet, communicate, and share new ideas to improve the home haunting experience.

http://www.hauntcast.net Listen to podcasts by Chris Baker--for haunt industry news, interviews, horror movie reviews and so much more.

Dover carries clipart and reference images for everything from architecture to costumes.

Drywall Compound, PVC Pipe, Paver Sand, Installation Tubing, Aluminum Dryer Hose, Gila Privacy Window Film should all be found in any major hardware store.

Halloween Props and Special FX Each year most major retail stores carry some sort of Halloween product displays of the latest props and special effects. As you are making your rounds for new additions to your collection, be sure to check out the craft and fabric stores at the same time. They also carry Halloween items. Don't forget the after Halloween clearance sales. This is a great way to add to your next year's prop arsenal without spending a whole lot of money. If you feel like shopping all year long for Halloween...there are many online shops devoted to Halloween. Doing a search for Halloween prop will get you started. One great resource is http://www.frightcatalog.com/

Cheesecloth can be purchased from most fabric stores. Some stores will sell it by the yard. Online searches for *fabric cheesecloth* will show many online resources for purchasing cheesecloth by the yard. One site example: http://www.hancockfabrics.com

Pepper's Ghosts TV FX any video with a black background will work as a video ghost for a TV. Check out the website www.howtohauntyourhouse.com to download Pepper's Ghosts used in this book. Here are some other places you can purchase TV FX for Halloween: http://www.frightcatalog.com/Halloween-Decorations/Halloween-DVDs/ and http://www.bigscreamtv.info/

Vinyl Sign Printing Do a local search in your area for Sign Printing. Commercial stores and groups use vinyl signs for advertisements and event promotions. The signs are waterproof and can be made to size. Vinyl signs usually have the option of grommets or rod pockets for hanging. Rod pockets are best, as they can be inserted with poles for easy sign hanging in the home haunt.

Credits

Font credits: Ravenscroft font was originally conceived and drawn by Tim McKenny, then refined and developed by Justin Callaghan http://www.mickeyavenue.com.

Photos by Shawn and Lynne Mitchell. All projects in this book were used by Shawn and Lynne Mitchell for their Halloween home haunt, *The Mitchell Cemetery*.

Index

VISIT US AT
WWW.HOWTOHAUNTYOURHOUSE.COM

ALL HALLOWS' EVE

*'Tis the night, they say
When all souls come back
from the far away—*

Thank You!

We would like to thank the following people for their help and inspiration in putting together of this book: Paul Venturella *(aka: Propmaster)* who first encouraged us to submit our video to his DVD collection after our very first home haunt year, from that moment on, we have grown and been inspired by so many like ourselves. We'd also like to thank FearNet for putting our little Cemetery in the national spotlight. They invited us to be one of 31 home haunts across the country for their new series, ***Route 666, America's Scariest Home Haunts***... A huge thanks goes out to all our fellow home haunters for reviewing our first, ***How To Haunt Your House*** book-
-Pete Henderson *(www.hauntspace.com founder)*, Paul Venturella *ww.halloweenpropmaster.com)*, and Deanna Griffith *(www.howloweenqueen.com)*, The Home Haunters Association Team *(www.homehauntersassociation.com)* and Chris Baker for interviewing us on his podcast, *www.hauntcast.net.* Special thanks goes to Ron Quijano for giving the book a once over with an editorial eye. Thanks to Betty Mitchell for lugging around the Halloween candy bowl and making sure all our trick-or-treaters got their fair share before making for the exit each Halloween. Thanks to James and Shelly Hull for showing up early and helping us get all the food ready before the party...it was a huge help! And we cannot forget all those who came out to visit us on Halloween night or to our Annual Halloween party...you are the ones we do it all for! For all your encourage-ment and helping us start a great Halloween tradition special thanks go to: The Hull Family (James, Shelly, Grant and Brook), Frank, Don & Pam, Pat, Buddy, Ron & Risalynn, Anne & Mike, Steve & Dodie, Clay, The Schneider family, Walter & Stacy, Don & Bernadette, Chester & Maryellen, Randy & Terri, Mel, Barbara & Robert, Kelly & Fred, Meghan & Robbie, Nancy & Sam, Bill & Becky, Shannon, Tim, and Mary & Barbara.